Health Savings Accounts: Steps To Lifetime Health Insurance

To Modify Obamacare, First Revise Medicare.

George Ross Fisher, MD

Ross & Perry Book Publishers
3 South Haddon Avenue
Haddonfield, New Jersey 08033
856-427-6135

Health Savings Accounts: Steps To Lifetime Health Insurance

Copyright © 2016 George Ross Fisher MD

ISBN 978-1-931839-69-3

. . . Also by the same author:

> *The Hospital That Ate Chicago*,
> Saunders Press, 1980

> *Health Savings Accounts: Planning for Prosperity*,
> Ross & Perry, Inc. 2015

> *Surmounting Health Costs to Retire: Health (and Retirement) Savings Account.* 2016

> *Pearls on a String: Further Extending Health (and Retirement) Savings Accounts*, 2016

> *Health Savings Accounts: Steps To Lifetime Health Insurance (This Volume)*, 2016

Ross & Perry Book Publishers
3 South Haddon Avenue
Haddonfield, New Jersey 08033
856-427-6135

Acknowledgements

For advice and support about the thrust of this much revised book, I owe new debts to the many people who read the first versions and commented. The first book was written as ideas developed in my mind, and rather in a hurry. The second revision was written, so later thoughts might be introduced earlier in the argument. This one was written and rewritten to rise above the twin possibilities that either, the Affordable Care Act would be completely repealed, or it would essentially survive forever. I still don't know its future, whether it is too big to fail, or too big to survive. Either way, I think it failed to reform some things which should be reformed. The best way to defend that position is to propose an alternative which is much simpler, but more radical.

Dedication:

To Senator Bill Roth of Delaware, who demonstrated the road between private and public sectors need not be a one-way street.

Table of Contents

TOPIC 333 Health (and Retirement) Savings Accounts: Steps To Lifetime Health Insurance 4
BLOG 3600 Privatizing Medicare 6
BLOG 3650 Modifying Medicare Early, Using It Later. 9
BLOG 3631 Pay/Go Becomes Prepaid 11
BLOG 3632 The Arithmetic Behind Our Claims, With Commentary 16
BLOG 3635 Imperfect Agency: HSA Administrators 28
BLOG 3651 Re-Arrangements and Addition of Childhood 31
BLOG 3581 Last Four Years of Life Reinsurance 33
BLOG 3551 Buying Into Medicare, Several Decades Early 41
BLOG 2773 Children, 0-26 44
BLOG 3220 Consulting Agency for Medicare Buy-out Issues 48
BLOG 3653 Transition Problems 51
BLOG 3636 Transition Issues 54
BLOG 3637 Reflections on Full Transition 57
BLOG 3487 Exit Strategy: Medicare as the First Pearl in the HSA Necklace 60
BLOG 3481 Health and Retirement Savings Accounts: to Privatize Medicare and Save Money, Too 63
BLOG 3652 Commentary 73
BLOG 3482 Questions about Health Savings Accounts 75
BLOG 3486 Suggested Additions. 78
BLOG 3648 Some Strategies in Reserve 81
BLOG 3483 Health Savings Accounts: Bare-bones Brief Summary 83
BLOG 3503 Traps, Pitfalls and Fallacies in Insurance Alternatives 85
BLOG 3504 The Subsidy Issue: Crossing the Line Between Private Sector and Public Sector 90
BLOG 3676 Epilogue, January 7, 2017 93

Health Savings Accounts: Steps To Lifetime Health Insurance

To Modify Obamacare, First Revise Medicare.

Health Savings Accounts: Steps To Lifetime Health Insurance

Introduction:

Without having such intention at all, I find myself writing a four or five volume essay on Health Savings Accounts. The HSA concept originated in 1981, with a letter to me from John McClaughry of Vermont, who was then Senior Policy Advisor in the Reagan White House. He had read my satirical book, *The Hospital That Ate Chicago*, and also was aware that Senator Bill Roth was working on a tax-exempt retirement fund, now called an Individual Retirement Account (IRA). John asked me if I thought two linked concepts might be of any value in paying for medical care.

Since it was exactly the idea I had been looking for, I began pressuring the American Medical Association, where I was a member of the House of Delegates. Executive Vice President Jim Sammons wrote me he had read my letter three times and still didn't understand "it". But one thing led to another, and the AMA endorsed the Medical (later, Health) Savings Account, firmly intertwined with catastrophic (high deductible) health insurance. The dual concept attracted the notice of people in Indiana and Texas, prompted a book by John Goodman, and was enacted into federal law when another Texan, Bill Archer, became Chairman of the Health Subcommittee of the U.S. House Ways and Means Committee. John McClaughry went on to run for Governor of Vermont, I went back to practicing Endocrinology in Philadelphia, while Health Savings Accounts with high-deductible insurance backup, quietly went on to enlist subscribers in the millions.

And Hillary Clinton emerged with her secret health plan, which I have been given to understand was mostly a national HMO, and later Barack Obama pushed his own version past an obedient Congress.

Many young physicians endorsed the motives of the Affordable Care Act, but most established practitioners hate the product. Nobody yet has satisfied me where it was planning to go. Meanwhile, although the dual Health Savings Accounts and catastrophic insurance saved 30% according to the American Academy of Actuaries, it was rather quiet about it; and still grew to thirty million subscribers. Originally most popular in Indiana and Texas, its present leading popularity is in New York and California. How bi-partisan can you get?

So, after discovering I was too old to be included in its coverage, I decided to write a book about it. The book's theme, as you might guess, was the age limits ought to be widened. Soon, a second book was needed to expand its horizons to retirement funding, and a third one to show how easy it was to link it to almost any other age group. The ACA bill got stalled by the death of Senator Edward Kennedy, Nancy Pelosi rammed the Senate version through without any mitigating features the House of Representatives might want to add, the reconciliation was never reconciled, and President Obama was stuck with it. So its flaws had to be examined. But then followed two bewildering Supreme Court decisions, the disastrous computer failures of the enrollment process, and the even worse failure of the Electronic Medical Record. Dr. Robert Wachter wrote a book called *The Electronic Doctor*, which describes how Mr. Blumenthal diverted thirty billion of the two hundred fifty billion dollars of Stimulus Package to mandatory "meaningful use" of the Electronic Record by doctors, now widely hated by them. For example, numerous fairly young physicians, including my daughter, her husband, and another comrade in a Philadelphia club, dropped out of flourishing practice before they reached retirement age, complaining they just couldn't stand it. The Obama administration tried to patch it up, but now it seems on the verge of collapse.

So, although you can see why I might want to write a book, it was unexpected that I could never complete one as planned. Some unexpected event would come along, invalidating some premise, and I was blocked from one attempted revision after another. The experience taught me just how wonderful the many hidden features of Health Savings Accounts really were, but it sure made it hard to write a book. And, although I twice started a second book the day after I sent the first one to the printer, approximately the same thing happened again. I discovered the HSA's roll-over feature (that had frustrated my hope to join my own plan) effectively solved a much bigger retirement problem. But I had to re-direct because Mrs. Clinton announced she was going to run for President using healthcare as a central issue, once again in secrecy.

As the reader will soon see, lengthening the insurance term limits causes a considerable cost reduction, I had to publish that. But immediately a Supreme Court decision upset my plan. Lifetime health insurance, I had discovered, is much cheaper than insurance in bits and pieces. But now, by golly, I find the possibility is very real for the Affordable Care Act to be thrown out by a new President. So, back to the drawing board. I decided to publish around Obamacare, rather than confront it. Reconciling the unreconciled ACA with Health Savings Accounts would have to become a project, not a book. Meanwhile, the public can evaluate what becomes possible for healthcare financing, if people just leave politics at the door and try to fix the problem.

George Ross Fisher, MD
Philadelphia. December 9, 2016

Health (and Retirement) Savings Accounts: Steps To Lifetime Health Insurance

If you are a fast reader, we begin with a five-minute summary of Health Savings Accounts.

President Trump has been elected. The problem of privatizing Medicare may no longer be how to find the revenue, it may be how in the world to arrange transition to a better system, gracefully. Those are two quite different questions. This book is an analysis of the first one (Is there enough money to cover a better system?): There just might be enough, but some toes would have to be stepped on. And toes might resist being stepped on.

But how in the world might we transition from pay-as-you-go, to total pre-payment? The transition from Medicare is clear enough; it's 100% government-run, it needs no transition if the patient dies, and no one has the courage to change it much, anyway. But in just what condition president-elect Trump will find the rest of medical care, is less clear. The Affordable Care Act has been going ahead, not so much hiding its details as avoiding frank description of them. Employer-based insurance no doubt keeps its components better informed, but treats future plans as business secrets; pending anti-trust suits about insurance mergers reinforce this protective instinct. Consequently, proposals for transition from the present situation are incomplete at best, and conflicting at worst. We're willing to make conjectures, but it takes more information to proceed.

Pre-payment generates tons of money for future use, but transition pushes huge Medicare expenses to the head of the line. No matter when or how things are changed by the new Administration, it will find elderly sick patients already in hospital beds, expecting to be paid for. The transition problem requires a clever navigator, but it will help to have sensible plans to choose between. The Health Savings Account offers both a long term solution and a fall-back for emergencies. But how to get from here to there will depend upon where we plan to go. Quite obviously, a bond issue might be used to cover early funding gaps, but beyond that, there need to be insurance re-designs to cover criss-crossing needs.

President Obama discovered earlier there were thirty million people with such wildly different requirements (prison inmates, illegal immigrants, mentally retarded, etc.) they didn't fit any one-size fits- all solution, no matter what had been promised for ordinary folks. President Trump is about to discover that is only part of the problem. Emergency issues requiring expedients will arise, early problems requiring bond issues and short-term solutions, perhaps; and then, medium term solutions for a decade of change, with long-term plans anticipating problems appearing long after he has left office. The system is so huge, mistakes are best corrected before they get out of hand.

Here are some blueprints, Donald. Good luck, Mr. President. Whether some citizens hate you, or some citizens love you, doesn't much matter. What matters is, we all need you to succeed.

Privatizing Medicare

Since Medicare finance isn't much affected by the Affordable Care Act, there's a short-term temptation to forget it. But its deficits and poor design are at the heart of the Medicare problem. At the end of this short book, the reader will realize it covers lifetime health insurance, except it leaves a big hole in the middle. Obamacare can only be absorbed after we see how much of it will survive.

*S*ince *Medicare finance isn't much affected by the Affordable Care Act, there's a temptation to skip over Medicare. But the ACA deficits and poor design frequently grew out of Medicare's design problems.*

Changed Circumstances. There have been three main changes since some wag called Medicare the third rail of politics – "just touch it and you're dead". The first change since 1965 is much-increased longevity as a consequence of much-better healthcare. Someone must have seen this coming, but apparently no one spoke up. Although prolonged retirement is expensive, notice also how it prolongs the period of time available for compound interest to work, so the income curve starts to bend upward after thirty or forty years, regardless of the economy.

Secondly, passive, or index, investing has greatly simplified and strengthened amateur investing. Finally, the Health Savings Accounts appeared, often producing savings of 20-30%. It's time to re-examine the assumptions of 1965, with these three lights shining on them: longevity, passive investing, and payment design.

Proposed. In "Ye Olde" Medicare, the average beneficiary pays $56,000 per lifetime (in payroll withholding tax and premiums), but now it actually costs the government at least $112,000 per person – the remaining $50,000 or so per person is secondarily borrowed, so there can be no left-overs for retirement. But prolonged longevity and longer retirement are inevitable consequences of better healthcare. Viewed in that light, Medicare is broke.

Our "New" Medicare, by contrast, seemingly would pay for all of present medical care, plus appreciable retirement cost, with the same revenue, no government debt, no rationing or curtailment of service. It does it without changing major program elements; this is a financial change, not a medical one. It really does let you keep your own doctor, and doesn't tell him how to treat you, because it doesn't concern such things. It just produces a financial design more reasonably parallel to the facts of life.

Tools Available for Transition to the New System, But Presently Not Used: 1) Gradual buy-in for latecomers. 2) First and Last Years of Life Re-Insurance. 3) Trust Fund Extension after Death. 4) Delaying the Start of a Childhood Roll-Over. 5) Flexible Retirement from Healthcare Residuals. 6) Scientific advances. All of these will be explained later.

Extra Tools, Needed From Congress: "Change the postal address of Medicare's Withholding Tax, and Premiums", so the same money, plus interest, ends up in the individual's Health Savings Account, at age 65. If a considerable surplus from compound interest then exists, the choice of buying out current Medicare can be an option. Re-depositing in an HSA makes such contributions tax-exempt and earns compound interest (we hope, at 7%) in an escrowed sub-account which bypasses current medical costs until it is time for Medicare. At least, escrowed in a way it cannot be diverted from Medicare use. Therefore, average payroll-withholding transforms from $28,000 ($700 yearly for forty years, taxable) into health care worth on average 18% more than that, or $825, because it's before-tax, and at 7% grows to $138,000 at age 65 (Try that out on your Internet compound interest calculator). That's what folks are paying right now, but it doesn't have the same outcome.

Starting at age 65, it then transforms $1400 yearly Medicare premiums, before tax, and thus really $1650 into 18% more for twenty more years, and also pays tax-exempt interest. (Most people will find they have to read this several times, because Health Savings Accounts are the only plan that enjoys these particular features.)The **net effect of augmented income tax augmentation, compounded, is to transform $56,000 before**

7

tax, into $534,000 before tax at age 84, the present life expectancy, not counting $112,000 borrowed by the government, which we hope they can stop borrowing. That doesn't sound like good arithmetic, but If you don't believe it is possible, just try it on one of the Internet's free compound interest calculators. (Furthermore, if an afterdeath trust fund is created to the limit of a legal perpetuity [one lifetime plus 21 years], the present expenditure is transformed by compound interest into whatever $2,066,000 is worth at the time, we should hope amply providing for all of Medicare, plus generous retirement without government borrowing.) You won't be surprised to find others think this is more than you will need. We will later suggest better ways to rearrange the same facts, but this is the general idea.

For transition purposes, it might be wise to create a contingency fund, of up to $250 at birth. But remember, the gap in a lifetime plan can only be finally addressed after we see what is to become of the ACA (Obamacare). For the purposes of this book, we simply treat the ACA as if it were revenue-neutral, a somewhat unlikely forecast.

Modifying Medicare Early, Using It Later

Pay/Go Becomes Prepaid

The mistake was made in 1965, but there was little choice.

The mistake was made in 1965, but there was little alternative.

In 1965, the originators of Medicare made two mistakes, both of which seemed perfectly understandable at the time. To get the program rolling, they enrolled my parents' generation to enjoy the benefits without charge, if they were already over age 65 (my mother lived to be 103). And for the same reason, they used current revenues to pay for such older people, who had never contributed to their own costs. The system was called "pay as you go" to justify taking current revenues to pay for benefits unsupported by previous contributions. Money flowed out as fast as it was received, but Medicare never made a serious effort to catch up.

Consequently, there was no interest paid for the use of the money, but the program did get started, years before it would otherwise seem feasible. The program is now over fifty years old however, and it still isn't paying interest on cash which doesn't get spent for decades. Furthermore, the health of the population invisibly improved so rapidly that decades were added to the lifespan of Americans, and the interest income being lost steadily increased, as well. Since everyone likes to live thirty years longer, pay as you go was considered a reasonable price to pay for it.

However, the possibility has apparently been overlooked that a transition to pre-paid insurance might only be mildly painful. And even if the transition proved to be very painful, eventually the cost savings of Medicare passed on to the subscriber, might be reduced by millions and millions. It is now time to examine whether biting this bullet could really be relatively painless any longer, and whether it would save much money. The answer appears to be Yes to both questions. To begin, the arithmetic will be skipped, and the reasoning

11

explained. Following that, the arithmetic is concentrated for those who wish to reassure themselves; it may be skipped by those who don't. If you get the reasoning straight, the math is easily checked by compound interest calculators on the Internet. If you do that, you may find the Internet calculators sometimes create some errors themselves, however, so check your fact-checking.

Medicare is partially prepaid by withholding roughly 3% of a subscriber's wages in advance, as can be seen on any pay stub. From age 25 to age 65, the money aggregates to equal about a quarter of Medicare's actual cost. Another quarter is repaid by premiums, from people actually receiving Medicare. Although the data is overwhelmingly voluminous, it can be found among the Internet reports of CMS, the Center for Medicare and Medicaid. Since patient payment revenues thus aggregate to only half of the total Medicare expense, the residual half is paid out of the general fund of taxes, and later borrowed to restore the fund. (Partisans might say it is laundered through the general fund before it is borrowed.) About 13% of our bonds are held by oriental foreigners, and most of the rest is loaned to American citizens. This is how Mrs. Sibelius explained things in her report on the Internet, when she was in charge of it. The accumulating debt is now becoming serious, even accounting for the slang phrases used in Congress, suggesting this debt can never be repaid. Stick it to the Chinese, except 87% of it is ultimately owed to U.S. citizens. And U.S. citizens would take most of the haircut, as another saying goes, if the debt were dishonored.

Now focus on an important feature of the average Medicare cost. As a total departmental cost, it includes every person who becomes eligible for Medicare by attaining age 65. It is not exactly what the average person pays, rather, it includes the whole program including those who pay nothing. Therefore, privatizing Medicare with the same funds would not deprive the indigent of anything at all; present funding already includes them. That's one of the main attractivenesses of "single payer", defined as Medicare for everyone at any age – it's essentially all-inclusive. Unfortunately, its deficit is all-inclusive, too. For present analysis it's a rhetorical advantage to say, any new system using the old money, would be all-inclusive as well. Except half of the increased cost causes a correspondingly increased deficit. At present, the annual deficit is about $200 billion a year.

It's also important to acknowledge that extended retirement benefits are an innate obligation of Medicare, and right now retirement costs aren't provided at all, except for the (older) Social Security program. Good care leads to a longer life, and we should be grateful. But longer life is expensive, and most people will find they have not saved nearly enough to make it comfortable. For this, there should be more sympathy than there seems to be. Nothing like this had ever happened before, so some skeptical people cannot be entirely blamed for wanting to see some hardship before they believe the government cannot borrow its way out of it. Financial crunch of some sort is surely coming in the near future, because we are recovering from a recession, a political party deadlock, and the threat of both domestic uproar and international discord, both at once. But the health care arithmetic remains pretty clear, as we will see in the next section.

At present, about half the cost of Medicare is recovered by the U.S. Treasury. Without paying any interest, the revenue immediately gets spent, and an equal amount is borrowed – that's what we just said. So to speak, we only propose to change the mailing address of the checks, that's what we also said. Just deposit that same money (in the same amount) into your Health Savings Account, get a tax deduction for doing so, and earn compound interest on the combined amount. With a tax deduction adding 18% in value, and transferring the money at age 65, it will in fact be more money than you appear to need, and it would certainly be less debt.

For the first time, it provides some retirement money "to compensate" for the extra longevity Medicare has provided. If you earn enough investment income (say, 7%), it will be enough to pay for the whole program, including indigents and disabled, so long as they are over 65 or entitled to a special Medicare disabled program, as 9 million already are. Remember, that promise includes a retirement fund. If you don't earn enough investment income, it won't cover it all but it will surely cover more than it would have, without any compound interest and tax shelter. And the investment return would probably be increased at the expense of the financial community, who will resist. Fee-only advice, rather than commissions, would add about one percent to investor

13

returns, according to the Wall Street Journal, although lobbyists for Wall Street vigorously deny it. The proposal here is to insist both systems operate side-by-side, until the difference is clear.

Although the arithmetic seems to be pretty evident, we do advise creating a contingency fund in addition, just to be safe. The contingency fund would have to be at least a hundred dollars at birth, and might be as much as two hundred-fifty. That's the only extra expense for a lifetime of healthcare and retirement which actuaries estimate to cost an average of $350,000 per average lifetime, plus an equal amount for retirement, to say nothing about the hidden elimination of the government's deficit for Medicare. That's a pretty good bargain, so we suggest consideration of paying some of the resulting surplus to a children's fund, rather than just letting it appear in estates. You can tell yourself you've helped little children, while protecting yourself against contingencies. The Medicare crisis goes away, the Retirement crisis is abated, the national debt stops expanding, and a start is made on the childhood problem – all with money you're already spending, plus a hundred or so dollars, just for safety and dignity. Read on, just in case you are good at math, and you don't believe in miracles.

By the way, it has been implied this release of money is due to inflation, and it is true the inflation assumption (for income and general expenses alike) remains about 3%. But the real success secret beyond any person's control, is inherent in the mathematics of compound interest. When investment goes much beyond thirty years in duration, the effective interest rate rises spectacularly; you can thank Medicare for that, if you wish, or perhaps Aristotle. Inflation raises your retirement cost, that is true. But it also raises your income, so at present it's a short-term wash except for scientific advances, which are surely a long-term net gain.

$400 at Differing Rates (Compounding)

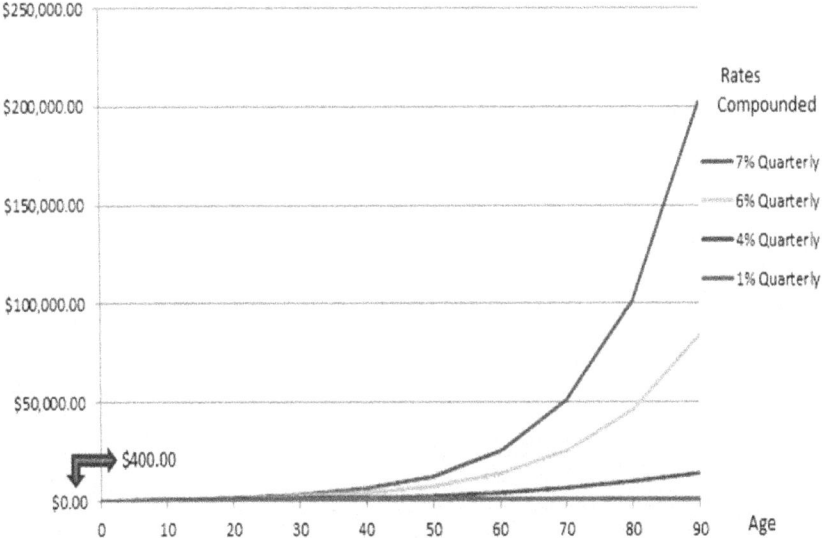

Rates Compounded
- 7% Quarterly
- 6% Quarterly
- 4% Quarterly
- 1% Quarterly

The Arithmetic Behind Our Claims, With Commentary

The average reader can check an approximation of these assertions in his head by assuming money at 7% will double every decade. More precision can be found by using one of the compound interest calculators found on Google. But be careful, since some of them have bugs.

Knowing how to calculate is less important than knowing <u>what</u> to calculate. Any computer's search engine has several free examples of compound interest calculators. It is also useful to know a few short-cut ways of calculating approximate answers in your head, just to keep check on computer calculations going off the rails. Be careful, because calculators can have bugs (or the computer's memory cache may not unload), but the commoner mistake is to calculate the wrong components.

The chief short-cut to know is a $100 fund of money earning 7% will double to $200 in ten years. Its related fact is, in fifty years a hundred dollars at 7% will equal (2,4,8,16,->32) times a hundred dollars, or $3,200. With compound interest, the result is not linear. The 7% in 10 years shorthand is a subset of the "rule of 72", which says you can divide 72 by the compound interest rate, to get the number of years it takes to double. So while 7% doubles in 10 years, 6% doubles in 12 years, 10% doubles in 7 years, etc.

It's true, $100 at 10% will double every seven years, (as in 2, 4, 8, 16,-> 32x) in 35 years, or to $3200, reaching the same value as 7%, but in fifteen fewer years. Our economy contains more examples of 7% interest charges, than of 10%. The difference between 7% and 10% is surprisingly great, and surprisingly meaningful in reverse. The 10% figure is often applied to impaired credit, or galloping inflation, and therefore higher rates are often a warning signal, not an opportunity. Approximations permit the reader to recognize anomalies, or to verify accurate calculations without repeating them.

Both approaches, short-hand and the Internet calculator, are recommended for verifying the following calculations, involving advance predictions which cannot be precise. One method of signaling approximation is to round off the answers to three or more digits of zeroes (2,400,000 is most probably an approximation, for example). We prefer fully calculated numbers, not to imply an accuracy which isn't present, but to allow the reader to follow arguments by recognizing components as they jump from line to line without elaborate identification.

Summary of the Math, With Caveats. This proposal is not free, it mainly substitutes investment income for government borrowing. The government thus benefits, but the patient benefits as well, because he ends up owning the investment. This is an essential feature, since without it the consumer may see the proposal as benefitting the government, without benefitting himself. The calculations are necessarily rough ones, and 7% may prove optimistic, but the system is self-balancing. Borrowing is reduced, so in the example the consumer gets the same product for roughly half its present net cost. "Roughly half" is approximate; the actual saving will be determined by market forces, both when he buys the investment, and later when he sells it.

To be explicit, this proposal involves passing early savings into the individual's own savings account, and immediately investing them. The consumer can measure his savings growth, and later can watch his own bills being paid with them. He keeps any savings for his own retirement, and even more if he is frugal enough to generate extra savings. Furthermore, he lives longer, which is largely only possible if his government has the money freed up to spend more billions on basic research to cure the diseases he might have died of. It is therefore possible to describe this whole system as a shrewd investment, growing out of cold, hard self-interest. Which, as the owner of the investment, visibly improves the individual's private benefit. So to return to the point we were making in the last chapter, hold off on ridiculing the idea of a newborn babe contributing money to it, it just looks that way at first.

To resume the arithmetic discussion, a deposit in a Health Savings (and Retirement) Account of $1650 [1] yearly from birth to age 20 (from diverted <u>Medicare premiums</u>) would result, <u>invested at 7%</u> in an escrow balance of $72,192 at age 20. If, at age 20, contributions of $825 yearly [2] for 40 more years (Source of revenue: diverted average <u>Medicare withholding tax</u>) were then substituted, both contributions firmly placed in escrow against college expenses and the like, might result in a balance of $1,260,000 at age 60. If investments realize less than 7%, this balance will be less. At age 65, 7% interest alone for five more years, generates a balance of $1,772,351. After subtracting a Medicare buy-out at age 65 of $134,000 [3] plus $30,000 (income tax), a balance is left for retirement of $1,608,351. That hypothetical balance could provide a pretty reasonable retirement fund starting at 65, and eliminate additions to the Medicare debt, and by age 84 (average life expectancy) still allow for extraction of $18,000 [4] to a designated member of the child or grandchild generation, at birth.

For persons in transition with less than a full lifetime to work this out, a **postmortem Trust Fund** could continue to earn interest from average age of death (84) to the legal limit of a perpetuity, dedicated to paying Medicare shortfalls even though the subscriber is dead, until the age of 105 [5] when further debts are extinguished. Meanwhile the $18,000 legacy recirculates in a child or grandchild's Health Savings Account, replenishing the fund for a new generation. It should be emphasized <u>this escrow fund is for Medicare</u>, to which major illness is increasingly migrating. (We here suggest Congress waive the Catastrophic insurance requirement during the sixty years when no medical withdrawals are being made.) Current medical costs for younger people, balancing the Medicare migration, should diminish, and be revenue-neutral for the lifetime system. In any event, they do not include either surplus or deficit from Obamacare.

This condensed example is given to answer the question: is there enough money in the system? There probably is, and the trick is to find ways of getting it out. The difficulties are political and cultural, not financial. Other programs can join the system like pearls on a string, so long as they individually remain revenue-neutral, or subsidies are created to make them so. <u>Success depends on achieving 7% returns from passive investing [6], and revenue-neutrality among newly added programs</u>. In a century, scientific discoveries might even reduce overall costs to the first year, and the last year, of life.

Footnotes.

1. For its own reasons, this is entirely credited to Medicare Part B, and Part A gets none of it. As a further twist, it is deducted from Social Security checks rather than billed.

2. The allowable amount is $700 per year, with an income tax deduction at the end of the year.

3. This is my own guess as to the probable buy-out price of Medicare, age (65) to average life expectancy (84)

4. The is the CMS estimate of childhood costs, birth to age 25.

5. A perpetuity is defined as one "life" plus 21 years.

6. My own portfolio averages 6.7%. I have it from John Bogle personally that 7% is a stretch, selected because of its calculating ease.

Comments.

It is not intended to follow this outline strictly. For example, the transition period to it must be somehow shortened, avoiding transitional bond issues whenever possible. One additional twist would be to take advantage of the population continuing to live longer. Half of Medicare expenses are devoted to the last four years of life, so the transition period can be cut in half by dividing the revenue into two escrow funds, one of which is funded by compound interest for 84+ years, and reimburses Medicare for the last 4 years of life it has already paid for. This cuts the burden in half for the second fund, a particularly useful feature during the transition period.

If the public will not stand for using old-age premium money to fund childcare, or if there is resistance to shifting obstetrics cost from mother to child, either the retirement must be reduced, or new sources of revenue found. If there is significant resistance to other generation-shifting of funds, it is usually less important financially than socially.

Without any government changes, passive investing is gaining on active investing, by almost a trillion dollars a year. The financial community can be expected to resist the shift to passive investing. Whether they will stiffen their resistance or adapt to the change, remains to be seen.

Further, if the ownership of index funds can be tolerated, perhaps a segment could be directed to venture capital funds for cost-reduction of medical corporations, or even to transforming medical industry profits into cost-reduction for its products. When the health industry consumes 18% of the gross domestic product, it must consider new financing methods if it is to avoid either government ownership, or a purely for-profit orientation. Perhaps healthcare could consider its place as an export industry.

In the meantime, healthcare must pay its own bills. Almost immediately I would establish a large force of accountants, to throw some light on central issues which are now conducted as either state secrets or business secrets. For example, I do not understand why hospital prices to uninsured patients are allowed to be so unrelated to their underlying costs, frustrating efforts to becoming market-oriented. Insurance companies have almost figured out how to protect themselves, but the public is appalled and unprotected. Perhaps the motive is protection of indirect overhead as a mechanism of cost-shifting. The only self-interested group I can think of are the trial lawyers, who base their settlements on "seven times the medicals". But I have trouble believing they have enough power over the state legislatures and judiciary to whip-saw the public into tolerating sixty thousand dollar charges which the insurance companies discount to six thousand, and the hospitals write off willingly, knowing their real inpatient cost is limited by the DRG[7]. And which I suspect cost the drug company much less than that to manufacture. If sunlight is the best disinfectant, let's have a lot of it.

7. Here, I am quoting my own personal health insurance EOB.

And I would like to see the true costs after taxes, of health insurance to various clients, particularly big business. It is possible to see two tax deductions, one to the employer and one to the employee, leading apparently to incentives for business to prefer high taxes on itself. There must be more to it than that, and one component is overworked congressmen. Each one of them has a million constituents, and spends a lot of time on the phone.

Estimated Cost of Medicare Buy-out.

The data in this analysis are usually condensed to a single average individual, in anticipation of use in individual Health Savings (and Retirement) Accounts. The number of individuals enrolled in **Medicare** (55,504,005), obtained from the Internet figures published for 2015 by Centers for Medicare & Medicaid Services (CMS), is divided into the total 2014 budget of the program ($373 billion) =**$6,720 Medicare cost per person per year for 20 years average** life expectancy at 65, or restated as **roughly $134,400 per person per Medicare lifetime.** As a check, Medicare cost is said to be half of lifetime medical costs of $350,000 or $175, 000. This is the ballpark guess of a Medicare buyout cost.

The accuracy of this figure would improve by excluding 9 million recipients under the age of 65 eligible by reason of disability, not by age. However, figures were not provided separately to distinguish costs of the disabled from the 46 million who became beneficiaries by attaining age 65. Assumed here to be roughly the same, disability probably costs more.

An important side point is not the exact amount of cost, but rather that **this composition includes everyone, rich or poor, who is over 65**. These figures therefore definitely include the indigents, and if anything include a disproportionate number of them. This should be attractive to single-payer enthusiasts, who wish to extend Medicare coverage to everyone, and who find that employing an extra eligibility based on age rather than income simplifies their task of persuasion. The calculations which follow are therefore not a "rich man's proposal" at all because Medicare is not a rich man's proposal. Its fault is being funded by pay-as-you go for several decades.

A second non-obvious fact of **regional variability** is readily inferred by comparing $6,720 per year (the overall Medicare average cost) with the $18,000 annual premium for New York employer health plans cited in the newspapers. Quite obviously New York prices are higher than those in a small rural district, but not three times as high. The New York employees, like the Medicare beneficiaries, must include a large subsidy of non-paying clients by paying ones, because of New York laws and demography, and are thus "conservative" estimates of revenue requirements in a limited sense. That the average is an overestimate is still further suggested by the $5700 annual premium charged for Medicare Part F for the highest income bracket, including a profit margin for the contractor. (Medicare sells coverage at wholesale prices and allows the Part F vendors to discount them, while still making a profit by constraining provider reimbursement.) Counting on the tacit reinsurance of the "risk corridor", some contractors lost money, but evidently not all of them did. It should be comparatively easy to calculate a more accurate estimate of costs by excluding under-65 beneficiaries, but the prediction-- that wholesale is less than $6720-- will almost certainly be borne out.

The underlying principle of our proposed example is equality with the present Medicare public charges. That's a rhetorical boundary, not an actual one. And an example, not a rule. Congress can set these charges where ever it pleases. Eventually, the charges must reflect an underlying need for them. For the present, current charges will suffice as an example.

*Current revenue comes in two approximately equal components. The first comes from the **withholding tax on employment of people aged 25-65**, the amount of which is specified as 2.9% of the wages, 1.45% from the individual paycheck, and 1.45% from the employer. From the Medicare annual report, it comes to an average of $700 per year for 40 years = $28,000. The other half, comes from the **Medicare premiums** (applied to reducing the benefits of <u>Social Security</u> checks by $1400 a year) from age 65 to the date of death, on average of 20 years = another $28,000. Some accountant should explain attributing all this to Medicare Part B, and why Part A is not attributed to hospitals at all. It seems entirely arbitrary, but you never know. Since contributions to Health Savings Accounts are tax-deductible, their value increases. We use the 18% flat-tax figure offered as a weighted average of real income taxes, so the HSA annual deposits are effectively $825 and $1650, ignoring the attributions. That's another example; does it make sense? To repeat, total average lifetime spending by Medicare is $6720 per year times 20 years = $134,000 ($2580/yr left for retirement). Is this a reasonable price for a buy-out? I doubt it, but even this figure is surmountable.*

Investment Income.

> ***There are two ways to increase investment income: invest the same at a younger age, or invest more over a longer period of time.*** *Depending on the sequence of investing, these previously collected sums should produce enough to buy out Medicare, with some left over to finance a moderate retirement – without increased debts to bondholders. Of course you can't spend it twice, but this is in an escrow account. The alternative is to have a separate account, and it is hard to say which is simpler. Although its internal distributions and cross-subsidies remain perhaps a little unclear, the over-65 retirement benefits are likely overestimated. The reader must weigh these approximations for himself, keeping one principle foremost. If the approximation does not comfortably dwarf the projection, it is too close for comfort.*

Transition Costs.

*In any event, the entire Medicare program must at most borrow $78,000 times 55,500,000 beneficiaries divided by 20 years of collection – each year – or roughly $200 billion of a 373 billion budget – **for transition from one system to a better one.** Moreover, alternative proposals for transition are suggested in later chapters. Even Wall Street veterans concede the U.S. Treasury has an outstanding reputation in bond issues for wars and depressions, so their advice is worth consulting. Once again, that figure is* *high to the degree the 9 million disabled on average have different costs than the 46 million elderly, low to the degree inflation becomes rampant, and largely unpredictable in sum. As far as frightened investors are concerned, the escrow rules should actually lessen the risk of panic illiquidity. Whether they see it that way or not, they are investing in the durability of the entire long-term American economy by investing in total stock market indices. It is safe to respond **the Medicare deficit is made wildly unsustainable by pay-as-you-go financing, whether privatized, or not**, and the proposed approach might actually help quite a bit. Furthermore, starting with a contingency fund of only $100 yearly from birth calculates to reach the same number with a little margin of error built in. But it includes no pension, and probably less elimination of debt.*

*The Health Saving Account law already provides potential revenue relief to the beneficiaries in two main ways: a tax deduction for deposits, and the freedom to invest deposits, tax-free, in any way agreeable. Furthermore, it collects no tax on withdrawals for medical purposes. (There is one exception which might be changed: taxes are not collected from medical expenditures, but are collected on HSA to IRA conversions.) Medicare, on the other hand, collects an average of $700 yearly for 40 years (25-65) in salary withholding, and $1400 a year for 20 years in Medicare premiums. That's about half its cost, another half is a deficit which must be borrowed. Using the rule of thumb of 7% doubling in ten years, an investment return of 7% in an HSA of the same money which resulted in an unsustainable deficit by pay/go, would be worth $825 per year (700 from Medicare + $126 extra value from the tax exemption) or $185,000 at age 65 (or even more, if Medicare costs are substantially less than $6720 for over-65 subscribers). That would buy out Medicare with $161,459 or so to spare, which after taxes would be $132,396 by subtracting the real average income tax of 18%. That much ought to provide approximately $8,000 annual retirement for the 20 years 65-85, the average life expectancy at birth. We can do better than that, but some money will have to be spent on the transition costs, so it's a maximum, **providing an individual HSA can earn 7% on its investment.** And worse than that if it can't. At least, we can sustain the point that, alone among health insurance programs, **HSAs transform any surplus after taxes into retirement income in the form of Individual Retirement Accounts, (IRA), and provides a way to generate potential surplus which is then likely to be under-stated.***

23

Future Projections.

It will be noticed we have left two features of HSAs unexploited, and one fly in the ointment unmentioned. In the first place, you have to be younger than 25 to take full advantage of what we have described, and you have to wait 40 more years to receive any tangible benefits. Secondly, the $3400 per year voluntary contribution deposit limit to HSA is unused and we suggest those who can afford it, spend it all on looming transition costs. These are both artificial limitations on the simplified example, a standing invitation to exploit new features. For example, look at what a hundred or so dollars would do, if deposited at birth. Of course you can add more, up to a $3400 limit per year. The result would probably be in the millions. Age and contribution limits should first be expanded, and the employment requirement eliminated. By expanding the time available for a recovery, these features would actually enhance the safety of the investment.

*An important stickler is, the law requires a high-deductible Catastrophic backup throughout the life of the HSA, but makes scant mention of overlapping insurance. When age and employment limits are removed, **this needs to be addressed by "or its equivalent", and possibly then more specifically,** since it leaves the HSA at the mercy of ambiguities its competitors can manipulate.*

The Importance of Solving Childhood Health Costs.

The HSA act was originally intended to appeal to young people, whose current medical needs were often small ones, and whose distant retirement looked utterly remote. Since the Affordable Care Act has considerably confused matters for this age group, we have decided to avoid discussion of the working age group, at least until after the 2016 Presidential elections give us some indication of where things are likely to go. <u>The proposal does cover Medicare, retirement and newborns – substantially everything except what Obamacare covers</u>. When the future of ACA becomes clearer, it will be necessary to write another book to integrate the issue of filling in such gaps. The HSA law does permit individuals to contribute up to $3400 annually to the accounts, but solvency seems temporary unless the age group 25-65 can produce a surplus to subsidize other groups. Here, we only contrast the HSA with about 100 to 250 dollars per year, from birth. That makes calculation easy, and small, but it grows relatively slowly and well might have to be supplemented at later ages, particularly during the transition period.

Let's be frank about projections so far in advance. They are meant only to distinguish areas where funds are "comfortably adequate" from other numbers which are more dangerously "barely adequate". The imagined precision is retained as a way of following particular numbers through the argument. Combining the two, a modest sum of $100 added to the account at birth would slowly grow to $542 (at 7%) by age 25. But that relatively small amount would be added to the withholding tax contribution at age 25, and even singly might grow to be $8,127 by 65. By age 84, without any withdrawals, it would grow (singly) to $31,450. **Combined with $825 a year** , however, starting at age 25 with $825 (withholding tax equivalent) added yearly, it would grow to $180,500 at 65, and subsequently without withholding tax addition, might **re-grow** (without withdrawals for retirement) to $166,000 by age 85. It would be in an escrow fund for Medicare, so it could not be spent for other purposes until age 65. There would be a withdrawal, however, to buy out Medicare at age 65, of $134,000. So the reduced value to $41,500 might re-grow in 20 years (age 65-85) to be $166,000. Using it up for retirement, however, would provide an annual pension too small to depend on for distant calculations. For the retirement to be a real incentive, it would have to last as long as projected longevity. The person would have to supplement it with private savings and investment along the way, a normal situation for rich people, but a frightening novelty for most people. Another step is required before such a lifetime venture is undertaken. Therefore, what is presented is not the best case. It will be improved upon later, especially with cutting the numbers in half with the Last Years of Life approach.

That venture would be a **rearrangement of revenue streams**. The earlier a sum is invested, the larger it will grow; in meaningful terms, it is worth far more for retirement if you start the same contribution twenty to sixty years earlier. In order to get the most out of the same investment, Congress might **remove the employment requirement and extend the age limits, both up to death and down to birth**. Maximum revenue could then be extracted if the financial equivalent of the Medicare premium began at birth, and twenty years later was followed by forty years of payroll deduction. Essentially, this means moving the equivalent of Medicare premiums to some form of trust fund, and re-directing the payroll deductions to the Health Savings

Account as described. These sixty years of investment leave five years unfunded, so if the Medicare age limits remain fixed at 65, the trust fund could begin as late as the fifth birthday.

Such rearrangement of the payment stream would generate a fund in the millions at age 65, allowing for much more comfortable slack in the investments, and supplying ample funds to transfer to a grandchild. **Funding the health needs of children is the greatest single unaddressed problem in all health planning.** It gets little attention because it seems so impossible to pre-fund the birth costs of a newborn. And it even stimulates mis-information, such as the mistaken belief that health costs of newborns are trivial. They are not as great as the cost of dying, but the financial resources of the parents are more strained. They spill over into grievances about the higher health premiums of women, in an era where feminism has had hidden effects on politics and even Supreme Court decisions. The transfer of Medicare premium funds to grandchildren has synergy with grandparent funding of obstetrics, and the Health Savings Account provides a vehicle to do them both. This particular caper is a political issue, requiring Presidential leadership; it is definitely not a financial issue just waiting around at the end of a lifetime of compound interest.

Any greater results would have to rely on additional donations to the contingency fund, or spectacular good luck in the stock market. This is therefore just about the limit of what a favorable arrangement could provide; except for outside contributions, any other arrangement would provide less. For example, switching Medicare premiums to fall between 65 and 85 (the current arrangement) would reduce the benefits by a third, as might a bad decade in the stock market. Suffering both reverses at once might wipe out all retirement benefits. But short of an atom bomb attack, it is hard to see how the average investor would lose money by doing it. Most of this plan requires changes in present law, although the growing national debt will create pressure to do something major to change the future trajectory of Medicare. The finance industry, already under strain, may resist. Consequently, the opportunities and drawbacks of Medicare Part F for employers also ought to be scrutinized, particularly as long as large employers recoup so much from their various unshared tax exemptions.

Long periods of unemployment could destroy this tempting dream, as could a protracted poor investment experience. The ordinary person would have trouble finding an institution which would accept amounts smaller than $100 without long-term contracts allowing the institution to trade short-term losses for long-term benefits. In the next section, we must therefore take a moment to reflect on the finance industry. And then we will return to this lifetime plan, by adding the Ends of Life approaches.

Imperfect Agency: HSA Administrators

Particularly if Congress amends the HSA act to broaden its scope, some serious thought should be given to establishing the rules for selling and administering the Health Savings Account itself. Just about all likely candidates have some conflict of interest which cautions us about distributing monopoly positions, or pay to play, as it is sometimes called, or nepotism as the form it sometimes takes. Nevertheless, when there are monopolies, kick-backs, formal or (usually) informal, proliferate at the expense of the customer, who then must "pay rent" for non-monopoly (arms-length or fiducial) behavior. It would be nice, for example, to feel if the customer detects churning or front-running, the customer would have recourse to some court, and not necessarily to have the issue foreclosed by involuntary arbitration agreements. A change in culture is always to be preferred to an imposed system of control.

The present structure traces back to the Constitution's Tenth Amendment, essentially telling the Federals they can deliver the mail, issue the currency, and police the borders, but anything else is to be conducted by state governments. In the early Nineteenth century, when corporations took their present form, that meant every new corporation had to have an individual state law, enabling and defining its rules. When it became obvious the proliferation of corporate charters made this system unworkable, states mostly converted to Uniform Corporation Acts, defining the rules for all for-profit and nonprofit corporations within the state.

By the end of the Nineteenth century, even this move toward uniformity became cumbersome for interstate corporations, and the push was on for uniform national laws, the Tenth Amendment be damned. The Civil War had discredited states rights enough to make nationalized corporations a viable entity. The first railroad, the Camden and Amboy RR in New Jersey, was given a perpetual monopoly on railroads in that strategically located state, and it took most of a century to untangle this complexity. Federal agencies slowly filled the gap for big corporations, but almost all corporations continue to start out small and state-regulated. So the result is informal flouting of the Tenth Amendment by the Courts, reaching out for a one-size fits-all solution. Strangely, the State of Delaware moved into this chaos with its Court of Chancery, to decide controversies where there is an obvious injustice, but no law exactly fits it. This history would seem to suggest that agents for Health Savings Accounts will have to be state-regulated, even though they grow from a Federal law. But if they are to be evaded, eventually another way will have to be found to make interstate HSAs viable and efficient. One thing standing in the way is the McCarran Ferguson Act, which lays out that no state need be hampered by the orders of any federal agency, concerning the "business of insurance." It does not improve the rest of the world's opinion of us, to be observed flouting our own Constitution.

We'll leave untangling this mess to others in the future, and concede that as long as HSA administration remains a small business, its regulation would speed along faster in fifty state legislatures, providing big corporations leave it alone and their lawyers ignore McCarran Ferguson. The consequence of all this is to relegate Vanguard, Fidelity and the rest of Wall Street, to the status of vendors to small businesses who in turn mainly respond to available services and fees without flagrant kickbacks to Wall Street, placing the customer's interest ahead of their own. If our arithmetic is accurate, the volume of business should grow into custodial accounts in aggregate of billions of dollars worth of stock certificates. But they would essentially remain small businesses, eventually requiring some nation-wide consistency governed by the House Ways and Means Committee and the Senate Finance Committee. And yes, some Federal agency to oversee the paperwork.

The structure outlined above has the effect of leaving the packaging of index and other securities to Wall Street, but the recommendation of which one the customer should buy, should be delegated to local small businesses or professionals. At present, computerized consolidation of stocks into an index stock, conducting an IPO, etc., are complex tasks requiring professionals, whereas the advice as to the best one to buy for a situation, is a mom and pop custodial function, requiring a small staff, a large lock-box at the bank, and a knowledge of customer needs. By and large, it requires no great talent to select among products (indexing took care of that), but in time it will require the talents of an accountant, and the integrity of a saint. Over time, these mom-and-pop small businesses will grow through franchises and other mechanisms familiar to business in general, and perhaps require a different system of regulation, with re-examination of the forces at work.

This overview of the probable business future argues for as much choice as possible. At the moment, we are being treated to the spectacle of brokerage houses violently resisting fee-only arrangements, so it is up to them to suggest a better resolution for the customer. Their eventual capitulation is not a foregone conclusion, they could drag out the change for quite a long time. Nevertheless, this business ought to explode if the middle-men took less of a cut from their monopoly, and customers could approach a 7% investment return with more confidence. Turning in the opposite direction, I find a doctor friend of mine is unable to retire, because a stock broker churned the trust fund account of her mentally retarded brother into extinction. The court question, of what sort of court should set similar things right for the HSA, should be settled early during the period when the decision between state or federal overall control, still remains fluid.

As a footnote, a reversal of fiducial requirement was slipped into the 2016 lame-duck period, so this issue must be quickly addressed.

Re-Arrangements and Addition
of Childhood Later

Last Four Years of Life Reinsurance

Half of lifetime medical expenses are reimbursed by Medicare. And half of Medicare represents the cost of the last four years of someone's life.

Half of lifetime medical expenses are reimbursed by Medicare. And half of Medicare represents the cost of the last four years of someone's life.

Having got middle-men off our chest, we return to a search for other ways to introduce greater efficiency into the medical financing system. That might be accomplished by reducing medical prices, or eliminating medical problems with research. Rationing, however, never seems to work without distorting resource allocation, and medical research is best left in the hands of the scientists. Here, we offer a third method, which is to increase the revenue by modifying its structure, while minimizing changes to the medical system it pays for. The National Institutes of Health (NIH) research budget is already $33 billion a year, and somehow that seems like enough. Right now, our mission is seeing what might be done with the payment system to fit its purpose.

Up until recently, paying for medical care has been treated as just part of paying for anything else, but it has some special features. For example, because of a welter of scientific advances, it is possible to imagine a future when nothing except the first and last years of life will contain any substantial medical costs unless they are self-inflicted to some degree. The American public seems consistently adverse to subsidizing self-inflicted conditions, which it views as a disguised form of suicide. Since homeless, addicted males seldom have children because females avoid them, non-cohabitation of the Lizistrata sort is a hidden way of punishing them for failing to support their families. With exceptions of this sort, medical care is an expensive need which will gradually become less essential. Except the system should be arranged to accommodate unexpected changes, because change itself is confidently expected to occur.

What's Reinsurance for the Last Years of Life All About? Ends of life concepts were designed to take advantage of the permanently J-shaped curve of medical costs increasing with age. They divide revenue into two investment classes maturing at different rates. The longer the period of compounding, the more we should want to save it for heavier expenses. (And the less we should be interested in spending a valuable resource on age groups with little to fear.)

Start by cutting **escrowed Medicare costs into two subaccounts, differing in content and thus in timing**. Overall, while all curves of lifetime health expenses are J-shaped, skewing progressively toward old age, containing roughly half of expenses in Medicare, and half of that (one fourth of total costs) concentrates in the last four years of life. (Later on, we will apply the principle to covering the increased cost of being born, addressing that initial upswing of the J.) There are six or eight variations, but our version has Subaccount A starting at age 25, the least expensive health year for the typical person, but also the time when Medicare withholding tax begins its forty-year climb. Our Subaccount B by contrast, begins at birth with a major obstetrical expense, but currently must abandon this opportunity to achieve maximum compounded interest because of a newborn's lack of income. (The age group from 25 to 65 is temporarily abandoned to the Affordable Care Act, until the nation decides whether to continue ACA, change its scope, or abandon it.) What follows is a description of financing everything <u>except</u> the Affordable Care Act, while temporarily accepting the implausible assumption ACA will seem revenue-neutral, until after the public gains full access to its books. The big data approach should speed up this examination.

Therefore leaving out ACA, and examining only what is left, Subaccount A buys out Medicare voluntarily, paying for retirement (which usually begins at the same time) with what is left over, in return for the hope of retirement income. <u>Subaccount B pays for the last four years of life,</u> thus removing half of Medicare cost from part A, <u>as well as funding one grandchild equivalent until he or she reaches age 25</u>. In effect, Account B pays for childhood, later materially helps buy out Medicare by re-insuring the last four years of life, and eventually becomes the basis for First and Last Years Insurance as a pre-paid substitute for pay-as-you go Medicare. It may take a long time to get there, but that's the goal. Meanwhile, it effectively cuts the cost of Medicare into two equal parts and thus makes it more digestible for buy-out. (By applying different revenue sources, its timing is different in the two pieces.) During the long transition period, the payments for Medicare are divided between the two funds to satisfy obligations, one of them is extinguished, the other continuing to fund retirement costs until the death of the subscriber. It amounts to shifting the costs and revenue around, taking advantage of longer compounding for heavier costs. Ultimately, it raises questions of how far the public is willing to go with all that, including donations to another generation, and being educated it's a sensible thing to do. By accomplishing many things at once, it acquires what mathematicians call elegance, but the public may regard it as too complicated unless it is accomplished in steps.

If, during the transition phase, there still remains a deficit, consideration might be given to establishing underline postmortem trust funds as a fall-back to continue the interest compounding until its debts are paid, and/or conceivably pre-birth trust funds anticipating childhood costs (see below). At the moment, mandatory conversion into an IRA would be subject to tax. However, we hope Congress can be persuaded to defer the taxes until the date of death. In this way, unpaid taxes could be utilized to extend retirement benefits until they are needed, and taxes can be discontinued if they aren't needed. Meanwhile, savings continue to gather investment income. During transition, there might be several revenue/cost mismatches which require expediency and/or bond issues, and there is no reason to see it as shameful.

When costs can finally be known, the Last Years fund reimburses Medicare.

The last four years of life are not the same as the last four years of Medicare. It is only possible to establish which four years are someone's last ones, after the date of death is known. The proposal here is to set one half aside as a special fund for the last four years of life, because old-age health

35

and retirement funds will generally not be needed for decades, but costs will eventually be heavy. When costs can finally be known, the Last Years fund reimburses Medicare. Some funds must be constantly consumed for medical care, and they should utilize funds which are soon to expire, and not be escrowed. Escrowed funds are usually set aside for distant medical costs, and like Odysseus bound to the mast, keep him from yielding to the temptation to use them prematurely. Meanwhile a third, non-escrowed, subaccount is free to manage current expenses, and need not be dealt with further in this section. Medicare doesn't know when you are going to die any better than you do, so it reimburses every cost at the time it is incurred, spending revenue about as fast as it is received. Account A was designed for future healthcare costs in all but the last four years, a burden considerably lightened by removing those last four years, and letting the revenue grow. The switch isn't exactly insurance, it is re-insurance. The beneficiary is then dead, and even his relatives would scarcely notice this transfer has taken place, except by auditing receipts.

As a matter of fact, Medicare needn't reimburse the particular costs for specific last-four-years clients, since there are only two parties directly involved, both of them insurance companies. By maintaining aggregate books, Medicare merely needs to determine the average cost for all its dying patients, to emerge with equal aggregate reimbursements for everyone who dies. Whether this bookkeeping short-cut can actually be utilized, however, depends on whether variations in regional cost are too substantial for local politics to tolerate. Even then, statewide averages might serve. This detail is an accounting efficiency which the two parties could sort out with Congress.

The substance of the following table is that the investment of $250 at birth would result in $21,714 cash for retirement at 65, plus the present value of $28,000 in Medicare premiums, plus an uncertain value for the improved structure. But this improved structure assumes no interest is gained on the premiums, and in fact they would probably be discounted to present value. So, it seems better to sacrifice the structure for improvement in cash flow. That would be summarized as follows:

<u>7%, From a Patient Perspective</u>

Account-A
(Medicarebuy-out+Retirement)
AGE...................25......(WorkingYears)..................65....................................85
      $0.00 $180,500 $0.00
          ←+$825/yr.withheld.x40→
                           (-$18,000.for.child)
                           (-$67,200 Last 4 Yrs.)
                           $95,300
                           ($78,146 (aftertax)
                           Retirement Fund

(Medicarebuy-out+Retirement)
AGE...................25......(WorkingYears)..................65....................................85
      $0.00 $180,500 $0.00
          ←+$825/yr.witheld.x40→   ←Prms.$1,650→
                           (-$18,000.for.child)
                           (-$67,200 Last 4 Yrs.)
                           $795,258
                         ($652,111 (aftertax)
                         Retirement Fund
                         (Minus Attrition)

Premiums First
AGE...................25.................45.............................65............................85
$0.00 $72,192 $289,219 $1,339,259
←+Prms.$1,652 x20→ ← $825 x40   →
                       (-$18,000.for.child)
                       (-$67,200 Last 4 Yrs.)
                       $1,254,059
                     ($1,028,328 (aftertax)
                     Retirement Fund
                     (Minus Attrition)

Account-B (Gifts)
AGE.(Birth+Chil...25.(Working Years).....................65............................85
$100+18,000 $542(-18,000) $8,127 $31,450

                          $31,450
                         ($24,690(aftertax)
                         contingency fund.

A number of combinations could be imagined from the premise that we should see what can be extracted from present contributions. And, of course other combinations are entirely possible if we relax that self-imposed limit. We attempted to show the requirements imposed by adhering to those limits and simply rearranging their sequence. You soon find that matching children with old folks defines the outer limit of revenue by rearrangement, the point where you have to add more expense to get more benefit. If it is deemed essential to adhere to present age matches, the benefit drops considerably. And conversely, if you don't aspire to increase the benefits, the cost goes down. No doubt the debate would begin to sound like a meeting of a condominium membership, with one half wanting to fix the place up regardless of cost, and the other half fearful of spending a penny they don't have to spend. Here, we defined the priority as revenue production, but other priorities must be considered.

> *Everybody is born, everybody dies, and nobody does either thing twice.*

Using different methods, it has been estimated by Michigan Blue Cross and confirmed by federal agencies, the average lifetime cost of medical care is somewhere around $350,000 in year 2000 dollars (i.e. corrected for inflation). The typical lifetime gain by the average citizen's new HSA is unknown, but seemingly approaches $1 million, if customers actually succeed in achieving 7% income on investment. It could be argued a total success of the HSA approach could benefit the economy by 9 percent of Gross Domestic Product, about half of which would benefit the federal budget. The sums we discuss are so large the considerations involve more than just health care, so as a physician I urge we restrain ourselves, for fear the medical advantages might get sacrificed.

Eventually, the taxpayer under present law might pay long term capital gains tax of 25% on withdrawals from tax-free accounts; revising such tax laws is under discussion. The present value of such revenue is difficult to estimate, but it would likely be offset by reduction of interest rates paid on the indebtedness, which is also hard to predict. And all of this would be offset by a long term rise in the stock market, also subject to capital gains tax. Since a rise in bond rates seems almost certain at present, and thus a long-term rise in stock market averages is likely, it seems reasonable to suppose the government would make a huge profit on an expanded Health Savings Account. Only a major prolonged recession or a war would reverse this judgment, and even that would see bond revenue mitigating the stock market loss. The private purchase of huge amounts of stock would certainly raise stock prices, and might put any qualms of the IRS to rest. It is true, stock market exuberance can lead to a bubble which collapses, but this observation never seems to restrain a bull market.

To review the matter, splitting Medicare payment into two escrowed subaccounts and one non-escrowed one, has simple purposes related to transitioning between systems, and really isn't that hard to understand.

1) Technically, it allows longer-term funding to avail itself of compound interest for longer periods, largely by devoting more attention to the matter, and ignoring the original assignment of the funds.
2) Secondly, a transfer of $18,000 out of a million-dollar retirement fund would not meet with nearly the same resistance as it would from a fund scraping the barrel to survive. We take this intergenerational transfer up in a later section, but here it should suffice to summarize, this transfer would solve a number of problems which hitherto have been treated as issues one simply has to endure.
3) Part of a spectacular revenue enhancement comes from adding twenty years of compounding a rather large sum ($1650 annually for 20 more years) onto the end of a long period (40 years) of compounding a smaller contribution, of $825 a year. Reversing the sequence (Medicare premiums first, payroll withholding subsequently) would generate even more revenue, and advancing Medicare premiums to childbirth-to age 25, would generate the most. Furthermore, any one of these sequences follows the design of original Health Savings accounts by ultimately depositing left-over funds into the individual's retirement account, as a sort of reward for being frugal. Acquiring revenue for other insurance components, what had previously been a unique feature of HSAs for retirement, it discourages early diversion of these funds to unrelated government activities (aircraft carriers, etc.), a recurring anxiety of beneficiaries. Perhaps more to the point, it gives the client a tangible reason to be frugal, at an age when such ideas are not entirely natural.

4) The proportions of the public who have already consumed, or paid for, parts of Medicare will vary with their demographics, largely related to the year they happen to have been born. But a rising proportion of cost in one compartment, means a decline in the other half. Because revenue often has unexpected connections to cost, this will always be a rough proportion, but it ought to help placate the sense of helpless public disenfranchisement which attends all major transitions.

5) And finally, this new configuration approximates the way things are probably going to go anyway, with ever-increasing concentrations of medical cost pushed toward the end of life. Not everybody dies at Medicare expense right now, but the universal trend is for people to die later, eventually making it approach 100%. Further, as we describe later, it provides a framework for first year-of-life coverage as well. That is to say, the trend is for health insurance to narrow down to the beginning and end of life, as science gradually eliminates disease. One day in the far future it might be said, nothing else is left of major health costs. Everybody is born, everybody dies, and nobody does either thing twice. Insurance as we currently think of it, will slowly become a thing of the past, replaced by what is more frankly a pre-payment methodology on a much grander scale. And eventually the public will see it happening, which eases political resistance considerably.

Buying Into Medicare, Several Decades Early

C ampaigning for President, Hillary Clinton brought up a proposal in 2016 to permit the uninsured to buy into Medicare coverage between the ages of 55 and 65. Eight years earlier, the Congressional Budget Office estimated such coverage would cost about $7600 a year per added client. The appeal is particularly strong for divorced women, because employer-based coverage ends when employment does. Nevertheless, the CBO estimate would make this segment the most expensive component of Medicare, so gradualism may have to wait for some enhancements.

It happens I was working on similar calculations for this book; the CBO estimate of what medical care once cost this 55-65 age group before 2008, seemed reasonable. The shape of the curve has probably not changed much in eight years. Nevertheless, there are now several reasons present estimates may be underestimated. The Consumer price Index for medical care has jumped around, but increased 3.4% a year, or over 30% more than the level eight years ago. Health insurance costs have probably exceeded overall costs for fifty years, so forecasting health insurance premiums has always included some guesswork. The cost curve for 55-65 is at the high end of a rising rate. Including more sick people also means fewer well ones, so there is a leverage. The data is based on aggregating claims data from still earlier years, so insurance costs tend to struggle to catch up with community costs. The cost of care inflates, but this portion of the population is at the high end of commercial coverage, so it probably escalates disproportionately.

In addition to statistical underestimation, there are probably invisible sources of confoundment. With Medicare just ahead, these people hold back on elective expenses, with lack of insurance exaggerating the tendency. If the experience with Medicare in 1965 or the ACA more recently, is used as a guide, we can expect a backlog of untreated gallstones, varicose veins, perforated eardrums and the like, to make an appearance once they regain insurance. That's quite different from pre-existing diabetes, heart failure or strokes, and will take longer to appear because it is more deferrable. It would not be surprising to find that post-insured costs are 50% higher than the 2008 CBO estimate, and will remain abnormally high for a decade. Finally, the method of data collection almost guarantees a low result. The published papers relate insurance companies were asked to report their claims, but no mention is made of insurance overhead, while the deductible and copayment ingredients are merely estimated. What seems to be implied is the data does not include insurance costs, probably for competitive reasons. And all of this is before we debate how much to subsidize, or how much it will encourage unemployment if we are too generous.

I surely do not know what is fair and proper to subsidize, and can see no good way to estimate it. Medicare is already financed by about 50% government subsidy from the general fund, as well as another 25% from payroll deductions, which have already been collected at a probably lower level. With inflation at 3%, a 3% payroll deduction is less than it seems. No mention was made of the revenue sources for this proposal, but hidden extra subsidies of $5000-6000, per person per year, would seem to be buried in it for someone to pay. While no one disputes the genuine hardship this group experiences, this proposal would only be a bumpy introduction to the practical difficulties of the "single payer" idea.

There is little doubt working women are handicapped in many ways by higher health care costs attributable to pregnancy, and this handicap results in a number of undesirable social consequences. My suggestion has been to shift the cost of obstetrics from the mother's insurance to the baby's, which usually amounts to saying they should be shared by the father's employer through the father. While this shift would have the undesirable feature of shifting costs from the working age group to a childhood group which requires some sort of to compensating cost-shifting, it mainly lengthens the period for compound interest to generate investment income, thus lowering the effective cost. A glance at the following chart clearly shows the bump in female costs between ages 15-45, transfer of which would go a long way to bringing the costs of males and females to pretty much the same level. Since this cost would ultimately be born by a transfer of surplus revenue from the Medicare group, it would heighten the attractiveness of First year of Life Insurance, which will be our next topic.

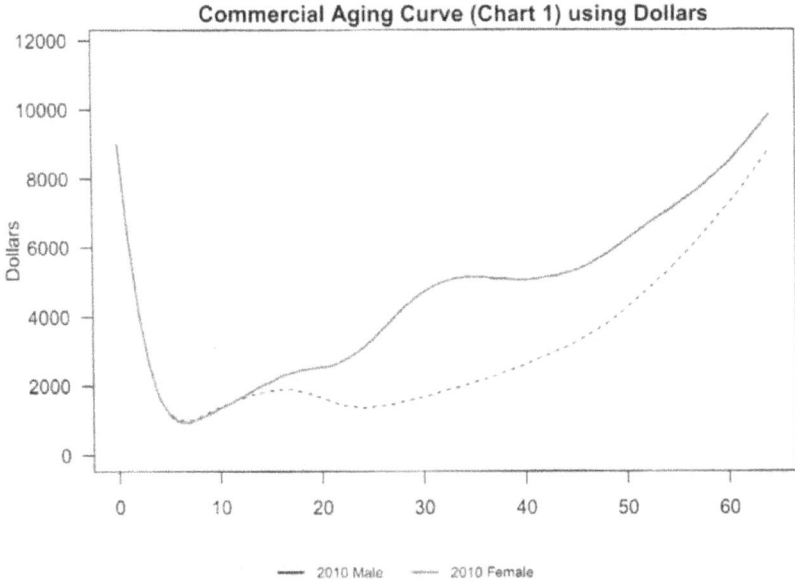

Commercial Aging Curve (Chart 1) using Dollars

Thanks to Dale H. Yamamoto. Health care cost - from birth to death.http://www.healthcostinstitute.org/files/Age-Curve-Study_0.pdf, June 2013. How much do people spend in total on healthcare over their lifetimes?

Thanks for the conversion to dollar values by George R. Fisher IV.

Children, 0-26

Everyone agrees there is a tangle of rights and responsibilities about the beginning of childhood.

*E*veryone agrees there is a tangle about the rights and responsibilities which begin when childhood begins. We wish to avoid this issue as much as we can, but partitioning the costs of the average child requires starting at some point or other, as its beginning.

Keeping the practicalities of paying for it in mind, we hope no one will object if we say childhood begins, the day you are born.

We next consider the healthcare costs of children, from birth until age 25, linked with the costs of the elderly, for a reason. One of the points made in this book is an arguable alternative to the present employer-based system, is to keep it within your family, rather than tax other people as a class. However, although the system now claims to begin with the first full-time employment, a newborn provokes about $18,000 of medical expense including obstetrics before that, right from the beginning, before the child can even feed him or her-self. Age 26 might be a reasonable place to begin self-support, not because of tax deduction, but since that's typically the age group with the lowest health costs. Even that starting age has its problems, because the parents are not much more accustomed to managing finances than the child is. The central question remains the same. Who is to supply the $18,000?

The Progressive movement started the idea of "family plans" about a century ago, but Henry J. Kaiser is credited with noticing an employer gift of the insurance would supply two tax deductions, the employer's and the employee's, during World War II. That "reduced" the cost of health insurance by at least 50% (for the employer and employee), but most of the time it made a married employee seem more expensive than unmarried ones, made healthcare seem a free cost to the recipients and therefore boosted its cost, introduced a religious note by discouraging multiple pregnancies, and was unfair to unemployed or self-employed persons who were excluded from getting the gift. It is impossible to determine how much this new twist distorted employment and medical prices, but by suspicion the unfairness was major. It surely prompted response, and this is one. If big business can get tax deductions for giving away healthcare, why can't everyone else?

So it is proposed – hold your breath – HSAs give the equivalent of $18,000 at the death of an older relative, to a newborn's HSA at birth. The average childbearing mother has 2.1 children, which works out to one grandchild per grandparent, and helps smooth out the cost of multiple children. Because births and deaths cannot be forced to coincide, some sort of fund has to be created to make all this come out fairly, but the result should equal a zero balance between two generations. And because everyone who is alive has somehow already paid his birth cost, there is less urgency to begin this feature at the onset of the program – it becomes a feature of the transition. And, going back to the pros and cons of including Medicare premiums in the compounding, the more surplus is generated, the shorter the transition period should become. Ultimately, of course, the cost of health insurance for the mother is reduced; but the main beneficiary of the transfer is whoever is now paying for the mother's health insurance. That would sometimes be the father, sometimes the employer, and sometimes the Affordable Care insurance.

A few children are cursed with horrendous medical bills, which quite often predict lifetime disabilities. For the most part, however, childhood medical costs are pretty small. It would seem to produce an ideal configuration for insurance, leading to mostly small premiums, affording a lot of protection against a fearful risk which is nevertheless relatively uncommon. However, a newborn is unable to walk, talk or feed him or her-self, beyond even mentioning his or her lack of savings. Parents are now expected to pay such bills, and when they are very large it is common for grandparents to help out. So it sort of fits the common situation to group the two dependent periods of life (childhood and old age) together, as a continuous loop skirting the income-producing period of life entirely. The underlying purpose is to shift overfunded money to an underfunded time, compensating the childhood cohort for the fact that compound interest appreciates very little during childhood, but very greatly toward the end of life. This configuration fairly shouts "risk pool" but that requires legislative action because it is more a metaphor than legal reality. It serves to explain to people why we have struggled to close the loop for twenty or more years, because what is true for children is definitely not true for Medicare, where the main costs congregate. To meet the disparity, we chose to employ patchwork solutions for a single generation, counting on the enhanced generosity of the public for disabled children to meet the major expense. This appearance contrasts sharply with the deceptively low average cost of ordinary childhood healthcare. The only danger is for this temporary expedient to become a career.

Please note the fiscal dilemma. Even if subsidies or gifts provided a $100 nest egg to start a health savings account at birth, 2.5 doublings at 7% would only create a fund of $525 by age 25. That's not nearly enough to fund healthcare for individuals at risk of auto accidents and HIV, while trying to pay for college, home mortgages or the like. By contrast, $100 a year <u>for forty years</u> might well pay for all of Medicare while retaining a leverage of eight dollars out, for one dollar in. Adding $1400 a year for 20 more years, would be much better, at 80 to one. For lucky people $8127 might work, but its safety margin is too narrow for launching a lifetime medical system. The actual plan proposed is a complicated variant of this approach. As the reader will see, there will be ample funds available for a lump sum donation, once the system has closed the loop, because just 8.5 extra doublings from the beginning of lifetimes to the end of other lifetimes, without supplementation, should silence any remaining doubts, at 256 to one leverage.

Once it gets under way, the two-generation process is very simple, requiring only a few amendments to existing legislation. <u>Extend the age limits</u> of catastrophic high-deductible insurance down to the date of birth, and wait for the premiums to <u>compound up to the date of death.</u> After that, <u>allow surplus Health Savings Accounts of the parents or grandparents to flow over to the HSAs of the child,</u> and allow surplus funds of grandparents and designated others to be transferred (from the date of death of one, to the date of birth of the other) via the HSAs of both. Gifts of this sort might even become a popular item in obituaries, in lieu of flowers.

Springing such a radically different proposal on an unprepared public is pretty sure to provoke ribald rejection, so it's gradually introduced here as a challenge to provoke alternative proposals. At the moment, I don't see what they would be. We are combining the advantages of two systems, for the young and for the old, which separately they cannot achieve, except through the socially threatened but biologically inescapable, concept of "family".

Consulting Agency for Medicare Buy-out Issues

Proceeding on the assumption Congress might authorize a system of Medicare buy-outs similar to the one outlined, some contractual obligations and procedures need to be established. Individuals need the opportunity to transfer payroll deductions, and later, Medicare premiums, in return for promising to re-direct payment to Health Savings Accounts to fund a buyout, and subsequently to do it. That's a single sentence, with several clauses. Essentially, since you can't move sickness to a different time, concentrate on moving revenue around to match the sickness.

As it happens, a conflicting principle emerges, that the **greatest revenue comes from investing the most money, in the hands of as young an investor as can possibly be chosen**. Remembering of course, that during transition some people are too old to start young. It reminds me, in reverse, of my father's observation the "best thing to happen, is to lose some money while you are young." At least, there may be time for a youngster to make up a loss, but it's still better if he also avoids losses when he is young. Making that choice favors both compound interest, and avoiding even the low health costs of the young. If the largest revenue source comes from Medicare premiums then it follows, newborn babies ought to be investing funds derived from grandparents on their deathbeds. Such twisting of original purposes probably will be motivated by knowing a dead donor will never notice. Supreme Court advocacy might argue the original purpose really was to finance Medicare painlessly, so this particular twisting results in the greatest revenue for the least complaints. The fact is, it is indeed advanced to take advantage of the greatest revenue for the least pain, but benefit is directed to someone who was largely unanticipated. And therefore the loyal opposition may oppose. We merely display the arithmetic.

If it is agreed the two primary sources should be Medicare premiums and Medicare withholding taxes, then the greatest revenue by sizeable amounts will result from assigning the Medicare premium source to age zero to age 25, followed as before by the Medicare withholding taxes, age 25 to 65. Gifts to the HSA, presently limited to $3400 a year to employed persons, should be accepted at any time, whether employed or not, and gift limits should be raised to encourage it. The potential is in the millions of dollars per person. If objections are raised by doing such a thing, the revenue could be substantially less. It will be interesting to see how this is dealt with.

Most likely, many individuals would get this choice during the 40-year period of payroll withholding, and request a payroll change after a few years of having partially paid in some other sequence. Should any portion of an escrowed account already paid, be refunded? A similar but different situation can be anticipated after age 66, when the question will be raised whether paid premiums should be repaid, but by that time the buyout should be accomplished. Since the two payment methods are of the same total amount, forty years for payroll deduction, and twenty years for Medicare premiums, the premiums are twice the size of the deductions. For present purposes, there will be some people who see that a bigger amount will grow at a faster rate and be a better investment, while other people either cannot afford the higher price, or else cannot live long enough to collect the benefits. So, if the sixty years of paying for Medicare are switched around, there will be five different twenty-year sequences with different prices, and different outcomes. Among the predicted outcomes will be better investments at higher prices, and worse investments at lower prices. Presumably, Congress does not want to get into the weeds of such details, but leaving it to the bureaucracy is the first step toward losing control. Congress needs an oversight subcommittee, but it also needs an executive body within the bureaucracy. Since there will eventually be a need for such a body, its skeleton should be started before the legislation is passed.

Each year of the transition will see somewhat smaller differences, some of which are inconsequential and some are not. If the cost and consequences of these entry points are worked out and explained, most people should have no difficulty recognizing their optimum sequence.

Quotas may have to be imposed to keep the system in balance, but in general a voluntary choice would self-select the best choice. Generally speaking, a larger deposit is most suitable for early selection and longer compound interest. If you are in your nineties, you may not care, or you may care a great deal. On the government side, it is in everybody's interest to have the transition cleared as soon as possible, with disputed choices referred to a specified court system.

Obviously, Medicare should be consulted about what it sees to be the most appropriate procedure, and in reply Medicare will probably describe some problems with starting Social Security in the absence of Medicare premiums as a deduction from Social Security checks. Again, a temporary transition team, with appropriate membership, should be established to iron out such issues. The number of clients involved strongly suggests there will be numerous unanticipated administrative problems to be resolved, so Congress should not allow the basic decisions to get beyond its control.

The donation of surplus retirement funds to infants poses a similar problem, triggered by getting the revenue from Medicare buy-outs. It would seem the creation of separate escrow accounts within Medical Savings Accounts might be the simplest way to keep track of this segregation, since the child would be expected to require its own HSA to receive the funds, and later to distribute them. There are likely to be a number of incompetent elderly and newborns, whose custodians would be arguing for negotiations, and more rigid uniform procedures. After initial transition problems have mostly been resolved, there surely will remain a need for a permanent consulting agency for clients, and a need for a special court of appeals. This all sounds like a lot of trouble, but comparatively simple when compared with switching millions of people from one program to another, and then listening to their outcries.

This isn't as hard to understand as it sounds. We return to it later, when resolving the Obamacare transition is actually before us.

Transition Problems

Transition Issues

Sickness costs have migrated toward the end of life, and will continue to migrate, as we have repeatedly mentioned. That's what makes pre-funding so attractive, but unfortunately the sequence is reversed for a simple transition, placing the biggest costs temporarily at the head of the line to be paid first, not last. If we can't fully afford one set of beneficiaries, we certainly cannot afford two sets on top of each other. For twenty years, people would be showing up for Medicare coverage, protesting they have either already paid for it, or have no means of earning the cost of it.

Bond Issuance. At first, there seems no way to cover the transition except by a bond issue of twenty or thirty years, and then there still remains the problem of paying off the bonds. Or waiting forty years for the revenue to catch up with expenses, a proposal which is unappealing to people who have to be re-elected before the fruit ripens. But both reactions are too dismissive. Eventually, there will be an enormous fund of money building up in the accounts, and therefore plenty of money to pay off bonds. Just when that will occur is a matter of complicated mathematics, but I hope I have convinced readers it will happen.

Voluntary. Therefore, it is at least essential to make the transition voluntary and perhaps a little unattractive for the first generation of beneficiaries who have already achieved Medicare eligibility, inducing them to shift some of the burden of transition (limited in the Medicare case to the escrowed funds) until later when the country can afford it. A quota system may even be necessary, but more probably the conservatism of old age will impel most Medicare beneficiaries to ask why they should bother to demand something they have already been given. The issue largely goes away in twenty years, unlike pay as you go, which stretches to infinity. And the funds required begin at only half of what they originally were, before removing the expense of the last four years of life.

But on the other hand, not every elderly person has ferocious medical expenses. The trick is to figure out how many there will be at each stage of transition, figure out what proportion they represent, and phase in the cheap ones first. That calculation, which is beyond my capability without dependable ACA data, will establish the point at which it is safe to phase in the expensive residual people. Or the sort of disorders it is advisable to delay. There's a risk in this, that the scientists who discover cheap cures will, instead, be overruled by the administrators of the drug and insurance industries, who feel their charge is to produce business plans to make a profit. That is, a combination of circumstances may thwart a fixed transition plan. At this point, our only hope is to use force, negotiation and pleas – essentially, to delay profits in return for enhancing them later. A dull and pedestrian refunding plan might then suddenly transform into a skillful negotiation of conflicted self-interests. Unfortunately, we must first determine the hidden costs incurred by the Affordable Care Act.

Cutting the Problem in Half With Last-years Reinsurance. A big hurdle is the group of people who are just stepping into Medicare, and an equal hurdle is the group just entering their last four years of life. Those people will cost the bulk of transition money, but have no way left to repay it after death. That's where the reinsurance to repay Medicare for the last years of life really serves a purpose, and the concept of post-mortem trust funds might have to test its viability, including any bad precedents it might set. Repayment would then be guaranteed, so there is thus likely to be less objection to removing it from transition planning. And if it is sufficiently foreseen, terminal care might already be pre-funded.

Staggered Transition. If, after we pay off both the first and last years of life, we then divide a lifetime of health financing into five twenty-year segments, it should be possible to complete the transition in twenty years. That assumes we start everything at once, placing everyone into the system simultaneously, at whatever stage the person's last birthday determines. That approach is pretty disruptive, as Lyndon Johnson discovered in 1965, but cowboy that he was just plunged ahead and ate the costs. His method was the one we are trying to escape, which is to adopt a pay-as you-go approach, and kick the can down the road. Eventually the borrowed interest cost builds up, and people start talking about never paying anything back. So, if a transition of even half of Medicare is too much to absorb, the transition can be further segmented, waiting for compound interest to build up in the last 4 years of life funds but holding off the number of transitions until it does.

If we do plan to start everybody's transition all at once, we must plan to pay each year as it comes along. That amounts to twenty mini-transitions every twenty years, because that's how people were born. Although we start with a plan which pays for itself, it does so by diminishing the cash cost through investing in total stock market index funds. Some years you make 20%, and other years you may lose 20%, but at the very least, taxing investment funds in anticipation of a financing gap before reserves build up.

Forty-year Transition Segments. Just to remind everyone, the evolution of this process over a century could be shown in a single table, which displays phases of a single life, with the exception of dividing the 40-year working period into two 20-year segments–except for the fact we cannot be certain how the Affordable Care Act and employer-based insurance are to be handled. That uncertainty segregates the low-cost age 25 to 45 segment from the somewhat higher-cost segment from 45 to 65; balanced roughly by increased income from salary raises, promotions, etc. The cost difference between the two segments will be heightened if the cost of obstetrics is shifted from the "family" to the infant, as we suggest, and shifted a second time from employer-based years to the retirement ones, when our plan finally reaches a surplus. The result is the virtual creation of two mega-segments which, combined, are roughly two segments of about forty years apiece, one low cost and the other high cost.

Twenty-Year Transition Segments. The contrasting advantage of suggesting a twenty-year transition is that each twenty-year segment has about the same cost, once the whole system reaches a steady state. That is, each segment is expected to borrow, as one compartment, the full income earned. Any shortfalls can be covered by segmenting the bond issue we mentioned. The medical cash costs will balance internally in each segment, except the first one must find the cash to prime the pump for twenty years. During that first twenty years the stock market has to behave itself and produce at least an average return. So that's the proposal to a lender: if we encounter a normal twenty-year market, the loan is easily paid off, on time. Otherwise, the loan must extend into a second segment. Selling the HSA program voluntarily to early adopters lessens the transition impact, but stretches out its resolution. If lenders rebel at these conditions, we await their counter-proposals.

So, what we are describing can be fit into a twenty year bond issue, but thirty years is more comfortable. It's a whopper, all right, coming to roughly a half million dollars for each of millions of people for several years, paid back over perhaps thirty years. At the moment, bond interest rates are at historic lows, so the timing would probably never be easier, unless some major diseases happen to find an inexpensive cure in the meantime. That's not impossible, but the longer we stretch the bond issue out, the likelier it becomes. Meanwhile, the population gets older, and expensive sickness is pushed later, too. In the meantime, we can expect a profit, from a spread between 3-4%, and the 7% we need to strive for, in the stock portfolio. This is an expensive buyout of a faulty system, but in the long run it should prove to be a sound investment, just by itself. We financed bigger issues in each of our last few international wars, so there is a good deal of history to review and consult about, with investment bankers. And consult with the Treasury Department, which does a very creditable job of funding bonds.

But the awkward fact remains, you cannot devise a comprehensive transition without knowing the true financial condition of ACA, and employer-based health insurance. Except for Medicare, so we start with eliminating the biggest hurdle first. You might discover this data with subpoenas, but cooperation is preferable.

Reflections on Full Transition

U p to this point, the reader has been exposed to a rather deadpan description of where available data seems to lead us. Experience with discussing the matter with friends at local clubs, has been the members of the audience either sit in bewildered silence, or they interrupt with imagined discoveries of flaws in the reasoning. Most of the interruptions are misunderstandings, requiring a lengthy digression to explain the point to someone unfamiliar with the particular topic which upset him. Since readers cannot speak out, but often have the same points of misunderstanding, let me pre-answer some common sources of agitation:

Some Common Misreadings. 1) "This is a rich man's plan, which does not focus on the poor man's problems." No, it accepts the ground rules of Medicare to include everybody, rich or poor, of a certain age; and we follow Medicare's data, so we accept their rules. The data per average beneficiary takes Medicare's data and divides them by the number of beneficiaries. Since Medicare data has age limits, not income limits, including 46 million persons over 65, plus 9 million disabled persons under 65, the average is probably somewhat more conservative (higher) than even the average rich man would actually pay, but the benefits are universal for the age group.

2) "Where is a poor single mother going to get $100 to start a contingency fund?" You mistake the purpose. The $100 is an example, not a mandate. It saves us repeating endless calculations for every year from birth to death. It illustrates the power of compound interest, implies that things which are entirely free are not taken seriously, and provides a point for subsidy, when subsidy is needed.

3) "These calculations are preposterous." You may be right if I have occasionally miscalculated or miscopied some numbers. But I tried hard to avoid that. The main purpose of the effort was to point out that increased longevity (caused by medical care) has brought the far end

of the curves into an area where the tail of compounding turns upward. We have long since ignored this feature, which greatly bothered the ancient Greeks who discovered it. Since the tail, except for the transition phase, of the curve stretches ahead nearly a century, we mostly haven't adjusted to the practicalities of the proposal, quite yet.

4) "Nobody can earn 7% in the stock market for extended periods of time." I looked over my own and some other accounts, and find I have averaged 6%. A recent article in the Wall Street *Journal* estimates that switching the stock manager to a fee-only arrangement (instead of a participation in the profits) would add one percent to the average investor's final return. If we get serious and exploit computers and other efficiencies, I have no doubt another percent investment return is feasible. Naturally, the finance industry doesn't want to agree, but that's the nature of creative destruction.

5) "What's the good to me, to wait nearly a century to get healthcare cheaper? The government or my agent would probably steal it, anyway." Yes, the problem of imperfect agency is a real one, and prevention must become part of the design. But the transition might take twenty years, not a century. Medicare itself was created in 1965, and you could have raised the same objection, then. You have to start somewhere, and you have to anticipate mid-course corrections.

The Real Practical Issues to be Confronted. At my age, I have no desire to start a company and make a fortune, so I leave that to my grandchildren. So I might as well be frank about the matter.

This plan cannot go ahead without some Congressional amendments. Not many, but sufficient to cripple the idea if it provokes opposition which has no motive except political ones. The age and employment requirements of HSA must be eliminated, and other government programs should be modified to adjust to changing life circumstances. Bare-bones catastrophic insurance should be standardized by some mechanism. If there were problems with the ACA, surely there must be flaws in catastrophic insurance companies, because they are accustomed to a one-year term format, and this proposal requires a longer horizon. A huge nation-wide system requires local offices and personal advice about how to handle changing investment environments, plus issues like investing for newborns, and for divorces. A totally new approach will require a lot of explaining, and all of this requires investment.

But mainly I have strictly left the working age group (age 25-65) out of the narrative, until the full facts are known after January, 2017 and we can learn whether it is to be revenue-neutral or regularly sustains a big loss. When Donald Trump gets control of the department and its books, I worry that deficits will prove to be far worse than even he thought they would be. His temptation to "expose the rascals" will be strong, but must be held back for better, more strategic, political uses. One important use would be to punish efforts to stonewall the new program. The Affordable Care Act took two years to emerge with regulations, Medicare in 1965 was an administrative mess for five years – their computers didn't work, either. So, it might be wise to start modestly, with the program of 1980 to which a few essential parts are added. Just for a taste of what's coming, read Robert Wachter's book, *The Digital Doctor* to learn how 30 <u>billion</u> dollars was recently taken from the Stimulus Package to finance the Electronic Medical Record, which eventually overwhelms just about every physician who must use it without crippling shortcuts. It often employs MUMPS, an interpreter language, largely given up as obsolete in 1985, so patching it is just about impossible.

So at least we don't have to usher in 2017 with a trillion dollar bond issue, after all. Let the program be voluntary, possibly with demonstration projects in various states. The secret of its effectiveness is that savings build up early for expenses which are greatest at the far end. But in a reversed transition, the oldest people must be served first, so you just can't afford to let an unlimited number of the older, expensive ones get in at the beginning. If we must have bond issues, let's start with patching up the cracks as they appear, and keep the bond issue from suddenly looming in the trillions of dollars. The best I can foresee is a twenty-year transition, during which there may be opportunities for wounded ACA supporters to get even. So let's be nice, and not be over-eager with eliminating all of ASA with a single stroke of a pen.

But let's not be timid, either.

Exit Strategy: Medicare as the First Pearl in the HSA Necklace

lacing a termination point for Health <u>Savings</u> Accounts was originally occasioned by recognizing the overlap created in 1965 by Medicare for everyone. At the time, it seemed pointless to be covered by <u>Health</u> Savings Accounts in addition to Medicare, and there was confusion with Health <u>Spending</u> Accounts with their "use it or lose it" features. Pouring remaining HSA surpluses into a regular IRA retirement fund, seems in retrospect the most effective way to create some incentive to save as much as you can in the Accounts. You couldn't lose it, and might well need it. To a certain degree, the size of the resulting retirement package is determined by the frugality of the individual client during his whole medical lifetime long before, but also during, the time he is on Medicare.

He would, however not be in the position of needing to do that, if he had been born earlier. The subscriber to an HSA could continue to deposit more tax-exempt money in the roll-over IRA for his retirement, giving the appearance of laundering it. Unfortunately, he would first have to drop out of the healthcare benefits, so he would lose the laundered tax exemption for health benefits on withdrawal. You would now have to view the extended tax exemption as repairing that unintended inequity. As Medicare began to be less generous, there were increasing gaps in coverage, and there may be many more in the future.

In what follows, we extend the retirement roll-over idea to several other medical entitlements without suggesting it be required as a universal rule. The time-honored old approach was to use an insurance surplus to reduce costs by recycling its surplus, but there are other things to consider. The first would be to imagine a theoretical sharp drop in the cost of Medicare, itself. Since 80% of Medicare is now spent on five or ten diseases, the possibility of a sudden cheap cure of one of those diseases is raised. The astonishing savings in the cost of strokes and heart attacks, created by taking a daily aspirin tablet – shows what it might be possible to imagine as happening again. Not to promise, but to imagine.

On the other hand, it is also possible to imagine less desirable priorities getting into the competition for such a financial windfall. Confronted with the issue, the average person would likely suspect such a windfall might as likely pay for aircraft carriers as Medicare deficits. But another opinion would emerge, and should be the default position. The Medicare program and its members had experienced the unexpected – and expensive – consequence of more protracted retirement than they planned on (five times as expensive, by one estimate). A more just assignment of such windfall would be to pay for the extra-long retirement cost it had provoked. If other emergencies seemed more pressing at the time, they could always be given priority on the money, but by default Medicare should first pay for its own consequences. In fact, nothing of the sort occurred.

In a sense, President Obama later created the same political problem for himself with the original budget for Obamacare. He did not need to make any speeches directing attention to the diversion of Medicare money to help pay for Obamacare costs, because plenty of Republican opponents were studying the budget. And plenty of Republicans remembered Richard Nixon's advice, "Watch what I do, don't listen to what I say." Having spoken to many groups of retirees about healthcare financing, I am acutely aware that retirees are watchful for any move to strip Medicare funds for Obamacare's benefit. It's about their highest priority.

And indeed their anxiety would be heightened by discovering Medicare is already 50% subsidized by general taxation, and then unsustainably maintained by borrowing money (selling US Treasury bonds) to foreign countries like China. And still more to the point, medical costs have been and will continue to migrate from working age people to retirement age people in the future. Just about everyone who dies right now, dies at Medicare expense. Even more than that, the effect of medical science has tended to eliminate terminal medical costs for people under 65, shifting them to people who get sick when they are over 65. It can be predicted a major cause of future Medicare cost increases, compared with the cost of living, lies in this shift of disease cost to the elderly. So it's a little hard to project whether Medicare costs will go up or go down, even if the cost of illness remains the same.

Recipients will change insurance compartments. Many attempts have been made to shift Medicare costs to the non-sick working population, such as through the payroll tax deduction and hospital internal cost-shifting, but the trend continues. A more sophisticated thing for the retirees to worry about, is the instability of a system which depends for its financing on that one-third of the population who are at work – but who are themselves becoming progressively more healthy – to support the medical finances of the other two thirds of the population, who are sick.

Taken in summary, there exists a great political opportunity for both political parties to put a stop to this "third rail of politics" talk. And to amend the Medicare Law immediately to provide that any declines in Medicare costs be immediately transferred to Social Security, for the purpose of paying for further increases in longevity. That provision should not cost much for some time to come. But the incentive it would give to the retirees to reduce their health expenditures might be considerable. Just as the comparable position Health Savings Accounts achieved, for whenever Medicare coverage was attained.

But its real benefit might be tested on that fateful day in the future. The day you pick up the morning newspaper and discover someone has cured cancer.

Health and Retirement Savings Accounts:
to Privatize Medicare and Save Money, Too

As earlier sections outlined, Health Savings Accounts were developed by John McClaughry and me in 1981, as a bare-bones health insurance scheme for financially struggling people. The package consisted of the cheapest insurance we could imagine (a high-deductible catastrophic indemnity plan with no co-pay features), attached to what others have aptly described as a tax-sheltered Christmas Savings Fund. That's essentially what you get if you sign up, today. What was this linkage supposed to accomplish? The Account part was intended for folks who must accept a high deductible to lower the cost of health insurance, but who then struggle to assemble the deductible. A <u>combination package</u> thus became the cheapest healthcare coverage we knew how to devise – the higher the deductible, the lower the premium.

As deposits build up in the account, the <u>remaining</u> deductible falls toward zero, **but the premium of the insurance does not rise** because the extra cost is excluded from the insurance part. At that point, you could easily describe it as "first-dollar coverage for a high-deductible premium." **Stepping through the process should clarify for anyone, how <u>expensive</u> it had always been to include the deductible costs inside the insurance!** It certainly compares well with so-called "Cadillac" plans, where the underlying motivation really was to include as many benefits as possible, money no object, with someone else paying for it and then writing off its cost against artificially high corporate tax rates – which were then eliminated by the healthcare deduction. If the government elected to subsidize our plan to provide it even more cheaply to poorer people, inter-plan subsidies could easily be arranged for seriously poor people, just as the Affordable Care Act does, by offering to transfer the same subsidy to it. Although HSA is itself absolutely the cheapest, neither it nor the Affordable Care Act is completely free of any cost, so additional features like charity must be supported by additional revenue from somewhere. Cheaper is simpler, simple is easier to understand. But cheaper doesn't mean free.

Last Years of Life

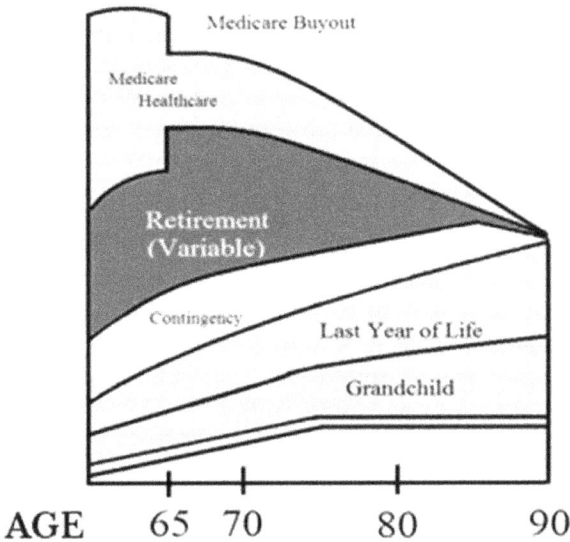

First-dollar coverage by any mechanism generates the danger of spending health money unwisely. **That undesirable feature was neutralized by letting subscribers keep what is left over at age 65, thereby generating (and greatly increasing) retirement income.** Retirement income is generally in short supply, and there may exist a future danger, that well-meaning attempts to supply generous retirements would destroy this incentive to be frugal. But right now it isn't a worry.

Other Incentives. One thing we didn't immediately verbalize was, making it a bargain entices people to save, even when they are sort of inclined to consume. We didn't think to include regular paycheck withdrawals, but that's another common savings incentive with proven effectiveness. Having loose cash does seem to create a vague itch to spend. But the Health Savings Account specifies an invitation to save for health care, using any surplus for retirement, a much more specific appeal. With that addition, it became a more attractive program, appealing to a larger segment of the population without reducing its appeal to the original ones. Our reaction was that everyone was complaining about high health costs, so the more people Health (and Retirement) Savings Accounts appealed to, the better.

The real game-changer was this: When a subscriber later acquires Medicare coverage, anything left in the fund is automatically turned into a tax-exempt retirement fund, an IRA. As enrollments in HSAs began to boom, it was realized this provision creates an unmatchable retirement fund if someone puts extra money into the account. I wish I knew whose idea originated that. So you might as well say **the basic package has three parts:** a high-deductible health insurance, a spill-over retirement fund, and a Christmas savings fund to multiply savings with compound interest – useful for both purposes.

It's amazing how many people think HSA has only one feature. It is **a double savings vehicle for two sequential stages of life,** with the tax advantages of the first stage getting it on its feet. The separation of the account from its re-insuring catastrophic health insurance, also identified the incentive to save, distinguished from a natural desire to share the risk like a hot potato. Adding compound interest adds particular attractiveness for the later stages of life, because compounding takes a long time before it means much. It connects two benefits end-to-end, lengthening the time for compound interest to become meaningful for the second one, as it would not, if it waited for retirement to begin. We eventually realized the deductible-funding and overlapped retirement-funding package, was the most attractive investment vehicle most ordinary folks could find. Beating it as a retirement fund alone was therefore nearly impossible.

Hence the double-strong incentive to save, sadly missing from every other form of health insurance. We strongly suggest adding this feature to Medicare, which badly needs some such incentive, although retirement is parallel to Medicare not sequential. Experience shows this unique set of double incentives to buy HSA was effective, so a 30% reduction in premiums for total health insurance began to emerge among pioneer clients, not merely claimed in theory. The recognition of all these advantages led millions of frugal people to sign up without an expensive marketing effort. Everything seemed to fall in place. Even though mandated coverage might have speeded up acceptance, slower adoption avoided the catastrophes of taking on more than could be handled.

So that's where HSA stands today – the best little health insurance idea available anywhere, unless someone monkeys with it. Even the remote possibility of getting very sick very often, was covered by adding the feature of a <u>top-limit to out-of-pocket costs</u>, paid for by dipping into a small portion of savings generated by other features. Anyone who thinks of a better health insurance plan than this one, is welcome to offer it. Every addition added to its complexity, but every feature added to its cost-saving.

Let's whisper a reminder to resisters: the policy is owned by the individual rather than his employer, so it doesn't suddenly stop when you change employers or move between states. To a different audience we could whisper, it could bring a second bad feature closer to an end, the business of paying for Medicare with debts which have to be borrowed from foreigners. The Account gathers interest, instead of costing interest. The best part is: it induces the subscriber to hold back from using the account, saving it for more distant requirements, which inconveniently come without warning. Paying for your old age is wonderful, but starting to save while young is vital, and more likely to work. Most plans now maintain an upper limit to the subscriber's out-of-pocket costs, protecting against a second illness with its second deductible. When we say, "That's all there is to it," we really mean that's all the advantages which have so far emerged. It's ready to be renamed HRSA, the Health (and Retirement) Savings Account.

Technical Amendments, Needed at Present.

Now, let's pick the nits, noticing how hard it gets to improve on it. If Congress could pass a few amendments, the following flaws could be more or less immediately repaired:

1) **Full Tax-Deductibility.** Attractive as it is, HSA still isn't as fully tax-deductible as the health insurance many employed people are given at work. The savings and retirement portions are indeed tax-sheltered, but unlike some of its competitors, the

high-deductible health insurance itself stands outside the funds (as what insurance experts might call re-insurance) and isn't covered. Employers get around this difficulty for their employees by buying the insurance themselves and "giving" it to the employees. Without monkeying around with this rather dubious maneuver to maintain tight control, we propose the premiums for the Catastrophic health portion of the HRSA might instantly become tax-exempt if the Savings Account paid the premium. That would appear cheaper for the Treasury, than proposing to make the whole package deductible. Because the other parts are already tax-exempted.

To permit something like that would require a one-line amendment to the HSA enabling act, but would restore fairness to the system, and bring out how much cheaper the Health Savings Account really is. Making it cheaper means more people could afford it, thus relieving the Treasury of the need to subsidize those people under the Affordable Care Act. That would compensate for some of the loss of revenue to the IRS of making the Catastrophic Health Insurance tax-exempt. Regardless of how the CBO scores this complexity, it should be remembered that poverty is not a lifelong condition for most poor people; after a temporary period of poverty, many if not most of them rise toward becoming tax-payers. Equal treatment under the law is itself a valuable asset; it could paradoxically be provided by lowering the corporate income tax, since many corporations already eliminate the corporate tax with the healthcare deduction. But that's not so self-evident, and politically hard to explain. If the Congressional Budget Office would extend its dynamic scoring to include retirement taxation on the HSA's eventual compound interest (instead of limiting its horizon to ten years), it would visibly be better to choose the compromise of letting the Accounts buy the re-insurance.

2) **A better Cost of Living Adjustment for HSA deposit limits.** There is presently an annual limit of $3400 for deposits into Health Savings Accounts, whose limits have seldom been raised very much. This new COLA should be formalized into a

continuing cost-of-living adjustment which is somehow related to the current rate of inflation in the medical economy, and perhaps takes account of a potential transition to HRSA by people over age 60. These late arrivals simply do not have sufficient time to catch up within the present deposit limits, even should they possess the savings to do so.

3) **Age Limits for HSAs.** It is a quirk of compound interest (originally noticed by Aristotle) that interest rates rise with the duration of investment. Consequently, much or most of the revenue appears after forty years, and consequently HSAs get more valuable with advancing age. To put it another way, young people contribute more time for interest to grow, old people must contribute more money to catch up. At present, HSA age limits are set to match employment, but the HSA will inevitably focus on funding retirement. Removing all age limits might go a little too far, but would substantially increase the amount of investment income generated, at almost no extra cost to the government. It might also supplement the platform for funding childhood health costs, a problem age group which stubbornly resists improvement. It might greatly enhance revenue for older subscribers as well (by reducing their health insurance cost), the surplus from which could be used at their death for the grandchildren generation.

> *Young people contribute more time for interest to grow, old people must contribute more money to catch up.*

First Years of Life

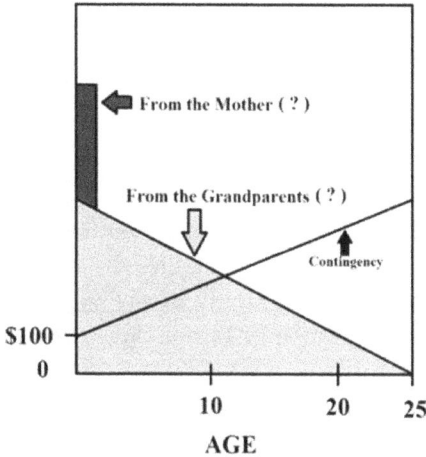

Extending the age limits would potentially also serve as a platform for re-adjusting dangerous imbalances in the healthcare financing system. We are fast approaching a demography of thirty years of childhood and education, followed by thirty years of working life, followed by thirty years of retirement. Substantially all of the revenue comes from the middle third, while the remaining two thirds of the population contain most of the health costs. To some extent this is unavoidable, but the whole health financing system becomes a dangerously unbalanced transfer system for well people to subsidize sick ones. It is possible to foresee the beginnings of class warfare, based on age alone. Consequently, society would be well served to create the more stable system of **subsidy between yourself as the donor and yourself as the beneficiary**. The alternative is to continue the process of having one demographic group collectively subsidize two other groups of strangers who generate most of the cost. Eventually this could induce well people to dump the burdensome sick people. I hope I am unduly concerned, but to extend the age limits for individual self-financing seems a very cheap way to begin stepping out of that particular mud puddle.

Finally, there is the conflict with inheritance laws. By extending the age limits for the funds to the legal boundary of perpetuity (one lifetime, plus

21 years), the ability to transfer funds between generations is enhanced without the perplexities of inheritance. It would be particularly useful to permit the fund to remain active until a grandparent's death, or even extend to the birth of the designated grandchild's 25th birthday. Like a trust fund, it could gather interest after the death of the owner, leaving the selection of heir to the last possible moment.

To return to the subject narrowly at hand, it is easy to see so many projects are made possible, you end up with an aggregate of goodies which eventually sink the lifeboat. Something must be chosen, something must be deferred, and the choice should be a delayed one, left to individual choice as much as possible. It can be commented in advance that retirement costs potentially dwarf sickness costs, and small single payments held at interest for long stretches have the greatest efficiency. There seems little choice but to constrain retirements to what the individual can manage independently, rather than permit retirements to absorb all the benefit of a new windfall. The theme is, and should be, one step at a time.

As an aside, it's true the subscriber to a Health Savings Account is not fully covered in his first few years, until the account builds up to the deductible. That makes a very good argument for starting the accounts while you are quite young. At first, that was a concern, but it has proved largely unnecessary to provide for it, among young healthy subscribers. Apparently, by the age hospital-level illness becomes common, ability to meet the deductible has mostly been achieved. Nor has it proved necessary to resort to sliding-scale deductibles hidden in the slogan, "the higher the deductible, the lower the premium" – probably because lower premiums immediately transform into more money for saving. These features might be reviewed when self-selected frugal applicants taper off, since HSA enrollment has so far attracted younger enrollees. For the moment, sales incentives seem adequate; everything else may be indirectly changed by HSAs, but very little is changed directly.

Future Expansions.

How far these three short amendments would extend retirement solvency, is hard to predict into the future, but it would be considerable.

Aside from any improvement never seeming like enough, it is almost impossible to guess the future timing of health costs, even when you can see them coming. But while the amendments might assure a comfortable future for Health and Retirement Savings Accounts, they do seem unlikely to address the full over-expectations of retirement. So the problem for many, many afternoons' deliberation, would be to expand the potential of HSAs until they become objectionable to competitive concerns. For that, I have four additional proposals which might work, but inevitably collide with professions who would be quick to suggest narrower limits. Let's describe them, meanwhile waiting to assess objections from those they would discomfit:

1. <u>A re-insurance scheme (insurance company to insurance company), called First and Last Years-of-Life Re-Insurance.</u> This has already been described.

2. <u>Medicare should be modularized</u> but without other basic change, so recipients need only buy pieces they need, using the invested proceeds for retirement. Obstetrical coverage immediately comes to mind. Sometime during the next fifty years it can be predicted at least one of the five most expensive diseases (Alzheimers, diabetes, cancer, psychosis, and Parkinsonism) will be inexpensively cured, once the initial cost increase is absorbed. We need a way to fine-tune the transfer of such medical savings into retirement income, understanding many competitors will hope to divert a windfall to themselves. Redirecting the Medicare withholding tax makes an easy way to channel the funding, as would reductions of Medicare premiums. Scientifically, Medicare is eventually destined to shrink as we find cures, but funding the resulting longevity must be given first call on the savings.

3. <u>The investment component of Health Savings Accounts should be dis-intermediated, partially if not completely.</u> Ibbotson reports the stock market has produced – for a century – 10%-11% long-term returns on large-cap stocks and less steadily, 4-5% on bonds, minus 3% inflation. You might not expect that, judging from the returns investors often receive; investors are definitely absorbing most of the risk. The volatility is much less than most people imagine, and there is every reason to

suppose Index funds of these entities should perform better with less volatility at far less cost, perhaps 0.1-0.3%. The days fast fade, when the public will continue to surrender the present level of stock market transfer costs and fees, which now sometimes erode investor return to as low as 1%. The fast-growing and simpler system is "passive" investing with index funds, and its goal should be an average return to the retail customer of at least 6.5% after inflation and costs. The struggle will be a fierce one, but the retail finance industry must re-examine who is at risk, and who is rewarded for taking that risk.

> *The wrong people are doing the medical commuting.*

4. <u>The center of medical care should migrate from medical centers toward shopping centers attached to retirement villages.</u> Architects report it will always be cheaper to build horizontally than vertically. Since we seem destined to spend thirty years in retirement, and the principal occupation of retired people is taking care of their own medical needs – the wrong people are doing the medical commuting. Teaching hospitals were located close to the poor, in order to use them for teaching material. But now "meds and eds" are fast becoming the principal occupations of high-rise cities. If there is ever a good time to place medical care closer to the patients, this is it.

And if ever there is a way to put the doctor back in charge of medical care, <u>decentralization</u> is the way to do it smoothly. We will always need tertiary care, but we don't need indirect overhead, skyscraper construction, or multiple layers of overcompensated administration. Even continuing-education is becoming a revenue center. No one can claim the present centralization made things cheaper, and the disadvantages of medical silos certainly call the quality issue into question. The Supreme Court failed us in the Maricopa Decision; so let's see what Congress can do with reconciling the Sherman Act with the Hippocratic Oath.

Commentary

Questions about Health Savings Accounts

Pertinent Questions: Three Current Tweaks to HSA.

1. Tax Equity. An alternative way to achieve more equitable taxation is to reduce corporate income tax rates, since the tax deductions for donated employee health insurance is a way of making health benefits cheaper for the employer than wages would be. And health benefits are a reason corporations pay so little of the published tax rate. Once benefits become equal they can be reduced, as eighty years have demonstrated. Tax equity first, then reduction, may be the best way to get corporate taxes reduced.

2. The transition-to-a-cheaper-system needs help, time, and more brackets for those who are already close to retirement. The private sector is inherently more flexible than the public sector in dealing with inflation, stock market volatility, and changing occupations. However, the public sector could readily be streamlined a great deal.

3. Longer durations for compound interest add flexibility and far greater returns without added cost to the government or client. In long durations, 6.5% returns rise far more rapidly than 3% inflation. This spread is an inherent feature of compound interest, and can be enhanced by lengthening the duration. The historic spread between the curves at 11%/3% underlined by Professor Ibbotson is astounding – and so costless it long seemed unachievable to shift its benefit a percent or two by John Bogle.

Pertinent Questions: Four Future Deep-Rooted Changes For Health Care, using HSA.

1. Although the whole-life insurance industry managed to accomplish it, a 90-year transition period is very difficult to plan for. As they say, life insurance is not purchased, it is sold. The last-year of life proposal cuts the transition period to a manageable size, thus providing funding flexibility from the start. The first-year of life addresses the otherwise impossible task of pre-funding the year of your birth – without help from somewhere. The present extended period of education before employment is being addressed by a declining birth rate, thus straining immigration policy. National defense alone argues this is an unwise policy to pursue in the present way. Luckily, the anti-perpetuity laws allow inheritance up to one life-span plus 21 years, an adequate period. The great danger in this is a revenue-starved government. Unfortunately, if public sector revenue became 100%, they would still claim to be starved, so their argument appears discredited. No strong argument is improved by exaggeration.

2. The public does not realize that Medicare is 50% subsidized, and therefore a single payer system aspires for the same treatment. We are already borrowing from the Chinese to pay for Medicare. As long as we have nation states, this is too dangerous to continue. Although Medicare is regarded as sacrosanct, anything which cannot continue will stop, one way or another.

3. The balance between the harmful effects of having a rentier class must be balanced against the harmful effect (of overtaxing them) on the incentives of elderly rich people. So the proper balance probably varies with the state of the economy. When two thirds of the population are to some degree rentiers, the situation must be approached with care. More retired people must be employed at home, while the finance industry must make more effort to prove its worth.

4. The business school and the law school are fast replacing the medical school as the preferred route to control medical care. The computer industry is not yet ready to join them. Controlling the hours and conditions of the workplace is not an acceptable route to

control of a service industry, and in the long run is self-defeating. The only way to gain respect from a professional is to be able to do what the professional does, only better and overall cheaper. Just how you accomplish that without going to medical school has not yet been explained, and "price fixing" is not an adequate description of its essence. The Professional Standards Review Organization (PSRO) devised by Senator Wallace Bennett of Utah comes pretty close, and although the AMA narrowly rejected it, reconsideration is recommended.

Suggested Additions.

S oon after the release date of the first edition of this book, an article appeared in the *Wall Street Journal* by Lanhee J. Chen and James C. Capretta of Stanford University, entitled *Instead of Obamacare: Giving Healthcare to the People.* The authors were in general sympathy with the Health Savings Account approach, and made three other suggestions with which I more-or-less agree. But they add a fourth which makes me unhappy:

1. Continuous Coverage Protection. They rightly notice many mandatory auto insurance recipients take out insurance, pay a single month's premium, during which time they obtain their driver's license. And then no further payments are made for the insurance. The authors propose higher premiums for those who do the same thing with healthcare insurance, but presumably waive the higher cost if insurance is continued for a full year. There are many people who are suspicious of making anything mandatory, but if it's mandatory, it's unfair to allow obvious loopholes of this sort to persist.

2. Medicaid Reform. The two commenting authors are evidently aware of the unsatisfactory quality of many state Medicaid programs, and propose splitting Medicaid into two parts, one for able-bodied adults and their children, and another for the disabled and elderly. Essentially, this is a rewording of high-risk pools, partially achieved by splitting Medicaid from federal plans. While this division might mesh more easily with existing workers and their families in the event of universal coverage (under a single-payer system), by itself it would not address much else.

A more useful split would be between inpatients and outpatients. That would match Medicare A and B, as well as the underlying Blue-Cross/Blue Shield organization of paper-work. Moreover, splitting helpless inpatients from ambulatory outpatients could surprisingly enable the marketplace to influence inpatient costs. <u>Since a large number of outpatient and inpatient services are identical,</u> it would establish a comparison framework for approximating inpatient to outpatient prices through a two-step market mechanism, which ultimately approximates market prices. For those inpatient services which have no outpatient match, a relative value system would provide a more stable way to set prices for the remainder of helpless inpatients. Doing this would close a loophole commonly employed to cost-shift inpatient costs to the outpatient area, resulting in vast confusion between two pricing systems for identical procedures. Hospital administrators would resist losing the ability to shift prices, so ultimately this is an argument about who is to dominate prices, the consumers or the providers. The "market" is a compromise between the two.

3. Medicare Reform. The main reason Medicare is often preferred to Medicaid is, it is potentially available to everyone regardless of income. But Medicare itself is 50% subsidized by the general taxpayer. No wonder Medicare doesn't need to mandate coverage. Effectively Medicare is subsidized more generously than Medicaid, and thus is the main source of healthcare deficits. You might subsidize Medicaid more generously, or you could apply a 50% subsidy to a single payer system. Either way will cost more, not less. Speaking politically, it is a question of whether you wish to offend the elderly Medicare patients, or the younger indigent ones. Essentially, Congress has already chosen sides once, and is unlikely to change its preference for current voters rather than potential ones. Finally, there remains one suggestion in the article which does make me uncomfortable, because of what it fails to say.

4. Retaining Employer Coverage. It still costs less to provide health insurance for employees, than to pay them wages and let them buy the same health insurance with what is left. Employers are therefore better off giving the health insurance as a gift, even though recent inflation has held back wages more than health costs. Presumably this anomaly would not survive tax reform, because employer-basing has turned into one big tax dodge.

But if it should survive, it presents the alternative to rectify the injustice to the other half of (small business) employees, whose employers usually cannot donate the coverage and then make it up at a spuriously higher corporate tax rate. Persisting eighty years after World War II which created the pretext, this is an unnecessary reminder of the many irregularities in the tax code. However, a one-line amendment to the HSA Law would suffice to extend the same tax exemption to outsiders, allowing other issues to remain dormant. This simple amendment would **permit the premiums of a catastrophic health plan to be paid by the Health Savings Account itself**, thereby extending its own tax shelter to HSA owners, at less additional commotion to the Treasury than full exemption. The present inflation distortion should not be missed as an opportunity to restore fairness, which almost everyone now recognizes to be nothing but a lobbying plum.

Some Strategies in Reserve

1. Temporarily forget about retirement funding, just finance healthcare. A smaller sum is easier to handle. I certainly hope this is merely a transition expedient.

2. Forget about death. Just keep re-investing the remaining money until its debts are paid off, and then have it terminate. The model is a trust fund.

3. Forget about childbirth. Start a trust fund in anticipation of having at least one child, and if you don't, provide for a legal contingency. The model is a "Bride's Hope Chest", which sometimes ends in funding spinsterhood.

4. Forget about living trusts. If you anticipate, or even want to anticipate, having children, start financing for it by saving money, investing it, and transferring it to its purpose without taxation of the transfer. But since we recoil at government ownership of the means of production, the model is a trust fund, not Socialism. Lawyers are uneasy about trust funds without living owners, so there must be a legislative approval of whatever we do that hasn't been done, before.

5. At present, we do all of our post-graduate medical education as "residencies" in <u>hospitals.</u> The consequence is twin silos with impaired communication. And then, our graduates (except surgeons) spend the rest of their lives working out of their <u>offices.</u> The consequence is the greatest flaw in the system comes from "hand-overs" of the patients from hospital to office practitioners who can't know what happened in the hospitals. The reverse is also true, from office to hospital, although it makes some sense to do a complete work-up when the patient is sick enough to warrant admission – as long as you also make it available to the referring physician. The reason behind this is the desire of hospitals to maintain a monopoly silo for the transfer of information, lest they

lose control of the patient himself. In Switzerland, almost all medicine is practiced in 15-25 bed "clinics", but that goes too far in the opposite direction.

One solution to this is to use retirement villages as half-way houses, with a resident in charge, under supervision, in an attached medical shopping center which also serves the retirement facility better. Naturally, the retirement villages resist that hospital control feature. A great deal could be done with tele-medicine that is not being done, but the idea flounders because of equipment start-up costs. However, when you see thirty billion dollars spent to patch this over with "meaningful use" of electronic medical records, you have to wonder how sincere the objections are. Because we don't have retirement villages well integrated into such a system, the extensive use of demonstration projects is advised, before the whole system is converted. In fact, it may make more sense to start with small rural areas than with large urban ones. Let a hundred flowers bloom.

> *If doctors get good at typing, they are spending too much time at it.*

6. My suspicion is the electronic record would make more progress if it were limited to laboratory, etc. data, and deliberately excluded doctor communication in favor of tape recorded communications or even video recordings. But not composition or typing. If doctors get good at typing, they are spending too much time at it.

In time, of course, this is a technical issue which will be solved. However, it exaggerates the time spent reading the stuff, so a major project of **automatic periodic summarization** is urgently needed. Presumably, that should grow out of an expanded search and retrieval system, which records whatever doctors have been interested in seeing, in similar cases, and at what stage. The basic fact is that if no doctor ever looks at it, it isn't worth including in the archive. Conversely, if doctors go after it like a dog after a bone, it should be high-lighted.

Health Savings Accounts:
Bare-bones Brief Summary

Health Savings Accounts

Enacted 2003. Subscribers as of Jan.1, 2015: 17 million.

Provisions: Briefly stated, any approved high-deductible indemnity health insurance plan, when attached to an approved tax-deductible savings account for the accumulation of the insurance deductible, or payment of other medical expenses. Deposits are limited to $3,400 tax-deductible annually, and are not taxable on withdrawal for medical purposes. Accounts presently may not be used to pay the insurance premium. The account is exchanged for a regular IRA at the time the subscriber begins Medicare coverage. (In this sense, an overfunded account earns interest until age 66 when unused funds are taxed but exchanged for any Individual Retirement Account which may then be used for any purpose. Up until that time, there is a 20% penalty for funds used for non-medical purposes.)

Suggested technical amendments: 1) Permit the account portion to pay the premiums for the insurance portion, making the entire Health Savings Account tax exempt. 2) Improve flexibility by eliminating age and employment limits. 3) Relax the deposit limits with a COLA and switch from annual limits to lifetime limits.

Suggested regulatory changes: 1) Limit costs and charges for deposits, withdrawals, and investment income to 1%, applying all the rest to the customer's account. The main purpose was not rationing, but to block expansion from Congressional intent of before-tax funding of deductibles, health expenses and retirements. 2) Permit subscribers the option to purchase index funds and take delivery on the certificates into defined escrow sub-accounts.

Suggested Areas for Future Expansion:

1. **First/Last Years-of-Life Re-insurance.** (To shorten the transition but extend the period for compounding interest, plus reduction of Retirement cost.) These four years consume 50% of medical costs. They are seldom paid by the patient himself, and affect 100% of the population. The present system is largely a transfer system to these four years, paid for by people who are not themselves sick.

2. **Study how the savings from future disease cures could be applied to retirement** (rather than mis-applied to battleships, etc) by flowing such savings into HSAs. The planning should contemplate eliminating Medicare gradually as its need disappears, a feature seldom included in the design of entitlements.

3. **Study the Dis-intermediation of HSA investing.** Privatization creates complicated agency problems, sometimes with excessive costs. Savings are possible from investing rather than borrowing, but the savings should reflect the risks better. The problem is how to invest several percent of GDP without using price controls.

4. **Decentralize.** Centralization of medical care has led to running it at great intermediary cost, unlike most businesses which become cheaper if centralized. Old people have most of the disease and do most of the medical commuting. The effective way to restore physician control is to decentralize from urban silos to suburban retirement communities. To do so gracefully, requires protracted planning. Begin with the *Maricopa* case of the U.S. Supreme Court.

Traps, Pitfalls and Fallacies
in Insurance Alternatives

As a general statement about insurance: it's a little surprising any of it works as well as it does. Most of us know the story line of Shakespeare's *Merchant of Venice*. It boils down to describing how a fairly decent merchant got into big trouble by pledging his life (in effect) to fulfilling the terms of his maritime insurance, which of course he never should have signed. There have always been terms of insurance no one should agree to, and no court should enforce; this was certainly one of them. However, there has long been a real need for maritime insurance, so over a period of several centuries an honorable, profitable and workable scheme was gradually patched together. Today it is possible for a shipowner with doubtful finances to make enforceable arrangements with insurers thousands of miles away, under terms of a contract written by shrewd lawyers, to pledge substantial sums derived in turn from investors who know very little about insurance, ships or navigation, to cover ships sailed by captains over whom they have no physical control, commanding crews who are often of the worst sort. It actually seems to work, if everybody involved is careful. And the same thing is true of health insurance. A workable system can be constructed, but some schemes forget their premises.

Regulations vs. Incentives. There was once a time for example, when the State Insurance commissioner was expected to protect the customer from claims against an insolvent insurance company. Insurer insolvency is a risk in buying any insurance. In recent years, however, insurance commissioners have appeared to have the main goal of protecting the customers from being overcharged. The two goals are in conflict, one pushing premiums up, the other pushing premiums down. Accounting procedures have grown arcane, dual systems of cost accounting are imposed, reserves are hidden. Many states require solvent companies to bail out an insolvent one, so an occasional slick operator escapes with a quick profit before the surviving competitors can protest. And so forth. When the state Medicaid program becomes an abuser it is difficult to trust the state's insurance commissioner to protect anybody. This resembles the environment which existed before the business community organized the non-profit Blue Cross plans. The deficiencies of service benefits and rising costs then seemed a small price to pay for a workable system. After a century, unfortunately, the employer-based system has trouble defending them.

Dread Diseases And there once was a time when newsmedia agitated worries about certain diseases, so Dread Disease policies quickly appeared, insuring against polio or cancer, or whatever else was in the news. When hysteria subsided, people dropped these policies, and the insurance company could legally walk away with unpaid claim reserves. As a matter of fact, much of the profitability of life insurance even today resides in expired policies of those who drop their policies; like exercise clubs for the flabby, who could never actually accommodate the number of subscribers they vigorously enlist.

It is not possible to separate insurance for the other stages of life, until you stabilize the ACA, since the employed third originates most of the revenue.

What Has This to Do with Health Insurance? Health insurance, being of more consequence to survival than exercise is, badly needs a system of multi-year coverage to protect customers from this hustle among others, And nowadays, against the same sort of dangers from government as it crowds itself into the health field, with eminent domain, escheat laws, devalued currency and just plain corruption. Unfortunately health costs are still too unpredictable to permit cost predictions over long time periods. We would greatly like to go from "term" health (and retirement) savings accounts, to multi-year ("whole life") ones, but the prospect of predicting health costs a century ahead, is too daunting for a major corporation which actually intends to pay its bills. Ultimately, almost all revenue for health insurance at any age, derives from the one-third who are employed. Therefore, it is not possible to separate insurance for the rest of life, until you have stabilized the ACA in some way or another, since that third originates essentially all the revenue to subsidize the other two thirds.

On the other hand, it raises a question whether employer-based health insurance would also be dropped by well persons who get into non-medical financial difficulties – except they mostly don't own their policies. Set aside the tax dodge and its inequity for small employers, prevention of employees dropping term insurance is still most likely the underlying purpose of businesses giving health insurance to employees. They want to make sure their employees are treated for illness before the business itself gets disrupted by absenteeism. They can't give lifetime coverage, because today most employees change employers frequently. It's important to see this motive is legitimate, because it must somehow be modified without the use of brute force.

Employees who own their policies might very well drop them, so the potential value of having insured employees with improved health must be balanced against its evident unsatisfactory features. As costs rise, at some point almost any IRS agent would question the imbalance of purposes. What seems to have tipped the balance was the discovery that tax exemption without loss of control could be created by giving it to employees as a gift, where the higher tax rate for corporations actually creates even higher tax exemptions for the employer than the employee. Times and attitudes change, but the argument that volume purchasing and other features secondarily make the health insurance cheaper for the employee seems to have been persuasive. The fact that non-union employees of competitors were treated unfairly, was highly unpersuasive until job mobility significantly increased. And converting high corporation taxes into high corporate tax deductions is increasingly seen to be just a step too far.

The time increasingly moves toward corporate willingness to surrender the tax inequity, with only unions belligerently opposed. The easiest way to accomplish it is for HSAs to be able to purchase it, since the rest of HSA is also tax-exempt. Employers might possibly prefer to use surrender as a bargaining chip in general tax reform legislation. At this point it scarcely matters which approach is adopted, either giving tax exemption to everyone, or denying it to everyone. In the present climate, giving it to everyone probably has the edge. The price of not extending the tax shelter to the catastrophic insurance portion of an HSA, is an unnecessary price for everyone who signs up for an HSA. The cost in Treasury revenue now begins to be less of a consideration than restoring fair play to the basic economy. Revenue can be restored by other means, but regaining a general atmosphere of equity is much more difficult.

Aside from this issue, catastrophic indemnity insurance continues to be confused with dread disease insurance. Let's insure cancer, but not indigestion, would be the general idea. One supposed alternative is: Let's insure illness, regardless of cause. But our goals have become confused; we should be advocating insurance against major health costs, regardless of medical cause. When you come right down to it, the underlying reason behind all this medical investigation of claims, is to prevent providers and patients from milking the insurance company. And a better way to accomplish that is to have the patient pay cash and be at subsequent risk seeking re-imbursement for his payment. The relative cost of the two approaches needs to be re-studied. In particular, it would be important to seek ways to <u>separate direct from indirect costs,</u> since the system of burying research in indirect overhead essentially makes research and teaching into beneficiaries of reimbursement abuse. In the outpatient area however, the experience of HSAs has been, the issue is not a significant one. For helpless patients in a hospital bed, a more sensible revision of diagnosis-related payment still makes sense.

Disability Insurance has been praised by some as an alternative to funding health insurance, and amounts to concentrating funding into diseases which entail extended disability from employment. It is true the really astounding health costs have usually included a big dose of disability rehabilitation, and in fact organized health groups have concentrated considerable attention to it. However, these efforts have largely been subsidized experiments, and they have yet to demonstrate overall cost-effectiveness, themselves. When teams of six to eight professionals devote up to two months to a stroke patient, the cost can be overpowering at any income level, and only 4% of stroke victims currently receive fibrinolytic therapy. Extending the same generosity to 96% of stroke patients would be ruinous to this approach. Important standard of care conclusions can only be reached when 80-90% are treated, at least in a few regions, followed by 80-90% rehabilitation, followed by observation of the cost effectiveness for some time afterward. You almost don't need to do the experiment.

When the net benefit to the patient is often meager, the question is whether the rehabilitation approach must change or disappear when the current research subsidy does. Extending it to helicopter and police rescue, we do not have even preliminary data to encourage this essentially rehab approach as a cost saver, but it certainly sounds expensive within the present state of the art. The current price of ambulance service suggests this is an area of considerable abuse. At a recent medical symposium on the topic, the audience was asked how many would prefer a disabled outcome in 30%, to dying of the disease, and very few hands were raised. These investigations must be conducted before final decisions can be made, but the early results are a warning. The advanced age of most stroke victims suggests this noble effort at best will not cause much economic improvement, unless the rehab becomes much less elaborate. We hope treatment advances will appear quickly, but national cost effectiveness changes are so far, only partially encouraging.

Home Health Care is also quite expensive, but most people would prefer it to institutional care. At the moment, home health care insurance encounters its main problems from government caprice. If Medicare cannot be depended on, or if a benefit can be removed at the stroke of a bureaucrat's pen, the finances of this sort of insurance will remain precarious. The retirement village is probably a more viable approach, because most of them are located in suburbs, and could also serve the suburb as a partial substitute for hospitals, with doctors' offices, laboratories and radiology serving a dual community. They are not cheap, but are probably cheaper than holding on to oversize, underused, private homes, inconveniently located for medical service. By far the greatest problem with out-of hospital settings is the instability of rulings by insurance companies and governments. Whatever problems the teaching hospitals may have caused, they have historically been reliable in this one.

The Subsidy Issue: Crossing the Line Between Private Sector and Public Sector

Although they seem to have the same design, **employer groups don't fit the ACA plan very well**. You will notice in current reports of 20% boosts in the individual health insurance contracts because of the Affordable Care Act, there was scant mention of employer groups. Their rates are negotiated privately, and usually at lower rates. They usually pay a different share of subsidies, too. In fact, it can be easier to deal with a plan with no subsidy at all, than with one which requires fitting several partial pieces together. Employer groups are often further subsidized by state and federal income tax deductions, with puzzling circular dependence. Employers make young employees subsidize older ones, while the ACA emphasizes rich ones subsidizing poor ones. (Young employees are seldom richer than older ones, so there's a mismatch, somewhere.) Young employees think of buying protection against unexpected illness, while older employees think of buying necessities at what they hope is a discount.

Some employed subscribers then find they are better off switching to Medicaid, which has historically been quite substandard. Others conclude their health risks cost less than the penalties for having no insurance at all. Some genius may be able to reconcile these issues, but at some point it seems better to start over. An important fact to remember: many poor persons are eligible for Medicaid, but haven't applied for it. That's a job the hospital social worker usually supplied in the Accident Room as they were being admitted. When it was decided to give ACA insurance to poor people, this awkwardness suddenly surfaced, in the form of implicit subscribers who were sicker than was planned for.

> *Mixing the subsidy with the service package usually causes trouble, lumping too many sick people with too few well ones.*

In the case of the Affordable Care Act, a fear is raised, a migration away of either subsidized or low-cost clients would raise the premiums of those who remain. The suggested compromise emerges that **if government subsidies are resorted to, they should be unwrapped from the service delivery package, and funded independently.** So long as the subsidy is distributed by the same criteria for everybody, it might pass muster. To emphasize: mixing the subsidy with the service package usually causes trouble; confusing too many sick people with too few well ones, has often proved to be a disaster.

Since Health Savings Accounts were begun independently of subsidies, they sometimes face the unjustified taunt they "do nothing for the poor man." If equal subsidies were distributed, the subsidy issue could become independent of the type of health care someone happens to have. It's too bad this wasn't examined from the beginning, since it definitely hampers the Affordable Care Act more than it helps it. Competition paradoxically does the opposite, no matter how hard that is to accept.

> *If you want to extend the same health subsidy to the HSA as is extended to ACA, go ahead, but stop using the addition of subsidy as a reason to prefer one payment system to the other, or one proposal to another.*

Our culture is reluctant to subsidize poverty, for fear of encouraging it. We are somewhat more willing to subsidize poverty caused by addiction, but prefer to subsidize it less than poverty caused by other diseases, like blindness – once again, because we are afraid we might encourage self-inflicted conditions. But hierarchy doesn't always stop with different diseases; we might prefer to subsidize one race, one region, or a whole host of other conflicting preferences. Nevertheless, it seems definitely better to subsidize individual poverty – as such – than to get into quarrels about the relative shamefulness of causes for health poverty, or the politics of their funding. My present conclusion is: if you want to extend the same health subsidy to the

HSA as is extended to ACA, go ahead, but stop using the addition of subsidy as a reason to prefer one payment system to the other, or one political party's proposal to another. Hidden in that preference is the delusion it is easier to control politics than the marketplace.

Perhaps, poverty should be treated as economists treat unemployment – a net absence of affluence, imitating unemployment as a net absence of employment. That says it might be temporary, which is not implied by saying it's a class of people, or a particular form of thinking. The Biblical description once implied both unemployment and poverty were two classes of society, quite likely permanent ones. But that was hundreds of years ago, and in a foreign land. A small demonstration program in several states might clarify whether this difference of viewpoint might actually lead to an improved subsidy approach. For a long while, I thought eliminating poverty would eliminate the sense of being poor. But it doesn't. Somehow we must get over the idea that the way we were born is the way we must remain, overlooking the plain fact that just about everybody is going to live thirty years longer, and that's generally a good thing. In fact, it's hard to think of anything most people would rather spend money on, than longevity.

Epilogue, January 7, 2017

Understanding What We Can Afford. My advice for early Presidential action would be to convene a group of accountants. They should acquire subpoena support, fan out, and tell us where health care stands financially, reporting back in six weeks. I trust experts know how to proceed, but would start with some recently-retired medical cost accountants. They probably already have an idea how things stand, and if retired some are eager to talk. Including a few actuaries and other experts would also be helpful. In a business merger, something like this would be called "due diligence".

The nation divides into three health groups **within a massive funds**-transfer system. While children and retirees produce **most of today's health cost**, they generate too little income to pay for it. Only the employed central bracket, aged 25-65, produces more income than expense, and they aren't very sick. (Savings by other groups don't count because their savings originate during working years.) Notice the Affordable Care Act happens to concentrate low-income sub-groups within the only age bracket which reliably produces **surplus revenue**, subsidizing the pre-employment and post-employment groups. Unfortunately, employer-based insurance also competes for much of this transferable revenue, by recirculating it. Consequently, it is difficult to guess how much is really available for subsidy purposes.

Both the Affordable Care Act and employer-based insurance have incentives to obscure their effects. The ACA hopes for an image of success, while employers recirculate potential tax revenue into multiple tax exemptions. So much, in fact, that few companies actually pay the high corporate tax they complain about, since taxes are a business expense, too. The public is thus unclear how much room is left to reform healthcare. The two subgroups who might know the answer are reluctant to share it.

The issue boils down to the size and elasticity of the potential surplus from working people, available to subsidize health costs of the other two thirds of the nation. If the surplus is small, our future should be one of cost-cutting. If it's elastic, perhaps we should postpone reform until there is greater recovery of the economy. If it's large, well, spend away. We will hear a lot of impassioned rhetoric in the next few months, but nothing will affect the decision as much as – understanding what we can afford.

> ***Eliminate Duplicate Coverages.*** *Returning to Health Savings Accounts, the existing HSA is adequate to get us past insurance collapses, even if HSA only gets a few tweaks of its limits. High deductible, non-copay, with a cap on out-of-pocket costs, is the most health insurance anybody ever needs. However, if an employer or some other program already provides more generous coverage, there is absolutely no sense in adding a cheaper insurance on top of it for the same coverage. Inflationary first-dollar coverage may have been a bad idea from the start. But even it becomes affordable for poor people by attachment to a tax-free Christmas Savings Fund, called a Health Savings Account. (Because you see, once the deductible builds up in that account, first-dollar coverage is effectively created, but the independent health insurance premium is unaffected. Frugal people will save it for retirement.)*
>
> *The rest of HSA is an expandable blueprint, to be implemented as circumstances and politics permit. It could amount to a few tweaks for the cost of living, or it could march through additional medical modules added to HSA like beads on a string, as they prove or disprove successive concepts. After all, the basic concept is this is a cheaper way to accomplish the same goal. If it doesn't reduce costs, why bother with it? Almost by definition, prisoners in detention for example are quite different from the mentally retarded for another example, and there are a dozen other such outliers. You almost never know if they mesh until you try to mix them. The people who lose coverage by ACA repeal are mostly refugees from a crippled Medicaid program, and they were eligible all along but didn't realize it. There is absolutely no sense in merging anything unless it works. The pearls on a string design permits the addition of new*

programs one by one, as they become urgent. They only need to break even after subsidies.

If Medicare gets into the trouble we predict, we have outlined a plan to transition out of it. There are thirty million people in some sort of offbeat situation, right now. If longevity should extend to age 104 as some predict, I believe HSA could adjust to it; if not, it must be modified. The investment management and "disintermediation" features seem to need re-negotiation fairly soon. Once it can be decided whether to remain state regulated, a minimal federal oversight structure could be created to acknowledge interstate sales are a modern requirement. There is enough money to do many of these things, but the political latitude needs to be tested. The essence is to rearrange them, and keep the savings within healthcare. There are lots of things to be done, without doing them all at once. The software industry, for example, should be able to get the electronic record into useful shape by eliminating physician notes until voice recording becomes usable, and when automatic summarization materializes. Everything worth-while has a cost attached to it, so creating a sensible accounting design is the first big step in medical computerization, anyway.

A final note on the net cost of adding new revenue. Astute critics will complain about (unmentioned) costs of catastrophic coverage. During the time Health is used as health insurance, of course bare-bones insurance is necessary to create stop-loss protection, because Medicare insures everybody over age 65, rich or poor. Some people are poor, so there will be losses. However, when the plan expands to Medicare pre-payment, there is no loss potential during the up to sixty years it is acting as a Christmas Savings conduit for later expenses. Consequently, there is no need to pay for loss protection during this interval. Whether you treat it as an escrow or a Christmas Saving Fund, should depend on whether it is at risk. Since at that stage the subscriber is not even a member of Medicare, Medicare is at no risk. I recommend removing high-deductible health insurance from HSAs unless they pay claims. Insurance is potentially unnecessary during the first sixty years of a Medicare reform, because the primary health insurances are expected to break-even (after subsidies) or be excluded. Thus, from birth to age sixty only custodial and banking functions are needed, describable as taking delivery of index certificates and storing them in a bank lock box, but more plausibly as part of an IRA.

Meanwhile, banks collect deposits and invest them, a function many banks or brokerage houses perform for little charge, making their profit on the float. It might cost something, but not enough to change the narrative.

www.ingramcontent.com/pod-product-compliance
Lightning Source LLC
Chambersburg PA
CBHW031300310326
41914CB00116B/1699/J